# CURRITUCK

# CURRITUCK

## DUCKS, POLITICS & OUTLAW GUNNERS

Travis Morris

THE History PRESS

Published by The History Press
Charleston, SC 29403
www.historypress.net

Copyright © 2008 by Travis Morris
All rights reserved

Cover design by Marshall Hudson.

First published 2008
Second printing 2008
Third printing 2013

Manufactured in the United States

ISBN 978.1.59629.497.4

Library of Congress Cataloging-in-Publication Data

Morris, Travis.
Currituck : ducks, politics, and outlaw gunners / Travis Morris.
p. cm.
ISBN 978-1-59629-497-4
1. Duck shooting--North Carolina--Currituck County--Anecdotes. 2. Currituck Co. (N.C.)--History. 3. Morris, Travis. I. Title.
SK333.D8.M665 2008
799.2'4409756132--dc22
2008018597

*Notice*: The information in this book is true and complete to the best of our knowledge. It is offered without guarantee on the part of the author or The History Press. The author and The History Press disclaim all liability in connection with the use of this book.

All rights reserved. No part of this book may be reproduced or transmitted in any form whatsoever without prior written permission from the publisher except in the case of brief quotations embodied in critical articles and reviews.

# Contents

# Acknowledgements

This book is dedicated to all the natives of Currituck County who have guided sportsmen and run hunting clubs; the women who have cooked the meals and served them; all who have farmed, fished commercially and driven trucks in order to make a living and live in their native Currituck County. The author has done all of the above except cook.

There are so many people in Currituck County who have guided sportsmen from time to time that I can't begin to name them all—in fact, I don't know them all. There are also several other people or families who have had hunting lodges in times gone by. Just to mention a few: the Wright brothers at Jarvisburg (Tommy and Jerry Wright's granddaddy and great uncles), Grover Sawyer at Hogs Quarter landing and Colon and Dorothy Grandy (Caroland Farm).

I want to thank Larry Woodhouse, Joe and Carol Lewark, John Barnes, the Merrell family (especially Jeanette), Olive Bunch Butt, Levie Bunch Jr., June and Mike Pell, Bobby Henley and Dot Whitson Henley, Wilbert Whitson, Wayne Penn and June Twiford, Randy Barco and Mike Doxey. Without the stories and pictures from these people, this book would not have been possible.

I would also like to thank Kaye Beasley, who is a real estate broker and works with me at Currituck Realty. When I can't find my daughter, Rhonda, I can always count on Kaye to help me with the computer. I'm not really computer literate. Kaye is a whiz on a computer and has helped me many times on all three of my books when I got stuck.

My youngest daughter, Rhonda Lee Morris, again agreed to help me with a book. She helped me with the last one, *Currituck Memories and Adventures*. I write it up in longhand. It takes me so long to type it up since I only type with one finger. She types it on the computer, edits, titles stories and gets it in the format the publisher wants it in.

Things don't go smooth. Rhonda thinks I should know everything she does about computer technology and I don't. We nearly come to blows sometimes, but it all works out.

Thanks, Rhonda.

# Why This Book Was Written

I have written two other books: *Duck Hunting on Currituck Sound: Tales from a Native Gunner* and *Currituck Memories and Adventures: More Tales From a Native Gunner*. These books were accepted so well that I felt like I needed to write another book. There are so many good, untold stories in Currituck that relate to ducks. I felt like more of them should be told for generations to come because Currituck will never be like it used to be.

Since the 1800s, wealthy people and captains of industry who could go anywhere they wanted in the world have come to Currituck, bought land, built hunting lodges and visited the area for one reason: DUCKS.

# Orville Leonard Woodhouse

Mr. Orville's son, Larry Woodhouse, was in my wife Jo Ann's store (J.I. Hayman's Hardware and Building Supplies) one day in July of 2007. He told Jo Ann he had a lot of pictures and stories he'd let me have if I wanted to write another book. I knew that Mr. Orville was on the North Carolina Wildlife Resources Commission for twenty-six years. That is longer than anyone else has ever served on the commission. I can remember when he entertained many people from high places by taking them duck hunting here. I also knew that Larry, being the outgoing person he is, could tell some good stories.

I met with Larry Woodhouse in his office on September 26, 2007, with tape recorder in hand. The following stories come from that conversation. Some of these stories could not be told if the people involved were not dead. Many of these stories will show what a big part ducks in Currituck have played in politics.

Orville Leonard Woodhouse was born of a farm family in Grandy, North Carolina. His father was Leonard B. Woodhouse and his mother was Louise Hayman Woodhouse. She was from Corolla and helped sew the material onto the wings of the first airplane, so she named her first son after Orville Wright. He married Ola Louise Aydlett on September 3, 1931. Miss Ola attended school in Poplar Branch. She walked to school every day—a long walk from their house—regardless of the weather. Her dog, King, walked with her every day and sat outside the schoolhouse until it was time to walk

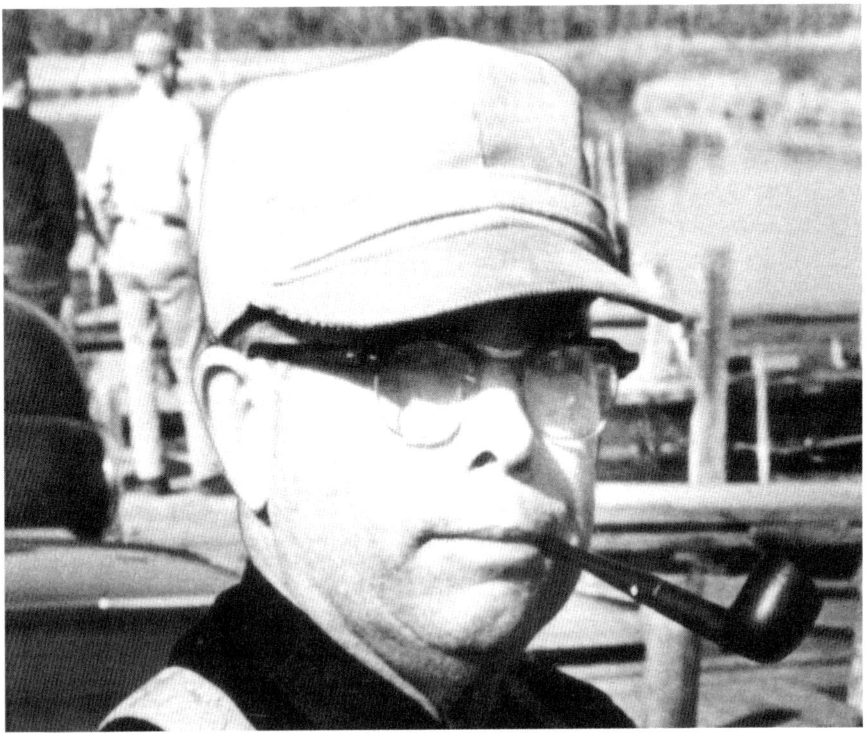

Orville Woodhouse at Neal's Creek Landing. *Courtesy of Larry Woodhouse.*

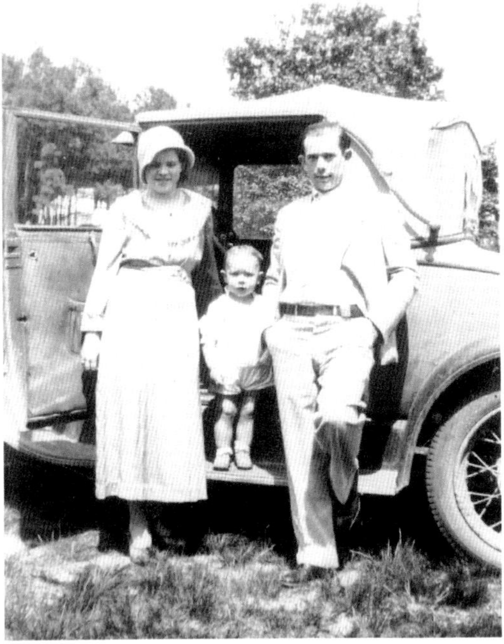

*Left to right:* Ola, Phyllis Rae and Orville Woodhouse. *Courtesy of Larry Woodhouse.*

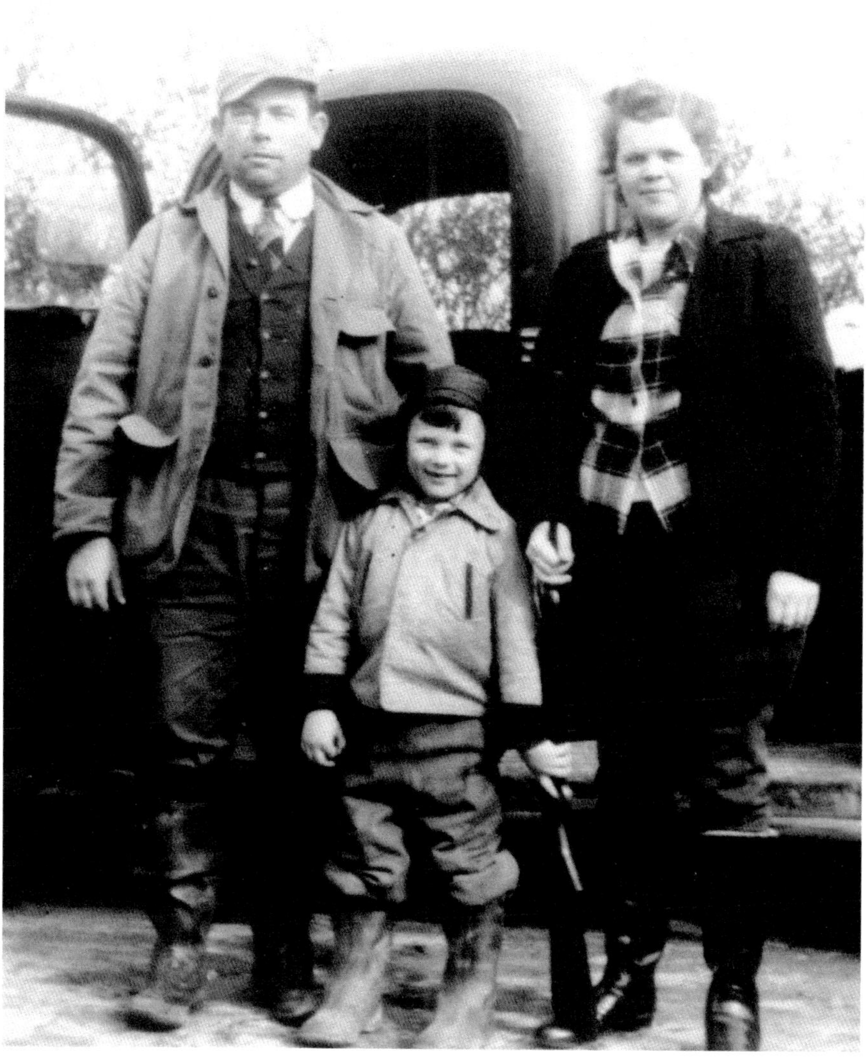

*Left to right:* Orville, Larry and Ola Woodhouse. *Courtesy of Larry Woodhouse.*

back home. When Currituck got school buses, Mr. Orville drove one. He stopped one day to offer her a ride to school and she said, "If King can't ride, I'm not riding." That ended that, but they dated nonetheless and got married the same year they graduated from high school. They had three children: Phyllis Rae, Larry and Rebecca. Ola's daddy was the Aydlett who worked at Narrow's Island Club. His brothers also worked there.

In 1931, the same year Mr. Orville graduated from high school and married Miss Ola, he went in the store business. He bought stores owned by

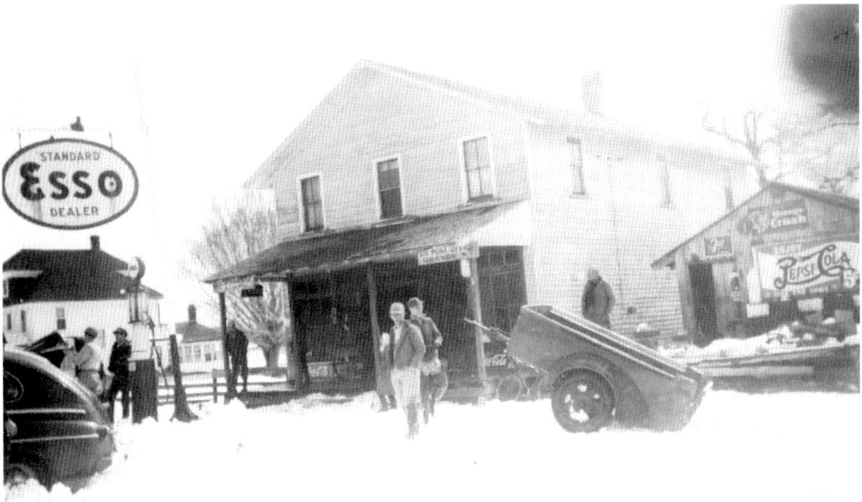


This is the Grandy store that Orville Woodhouse ran for fourteen years. This picture was taken in 1948. *Courtesy of Larry Woodhouse.*

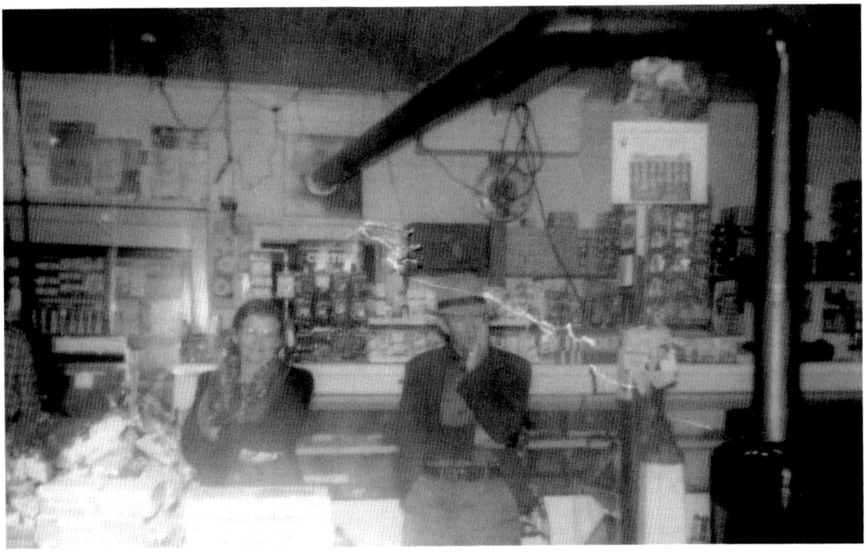

Sally and Ike Aydlett, Ola Woodhouse's parents. *Courtesy of Larry Woodhouse.*

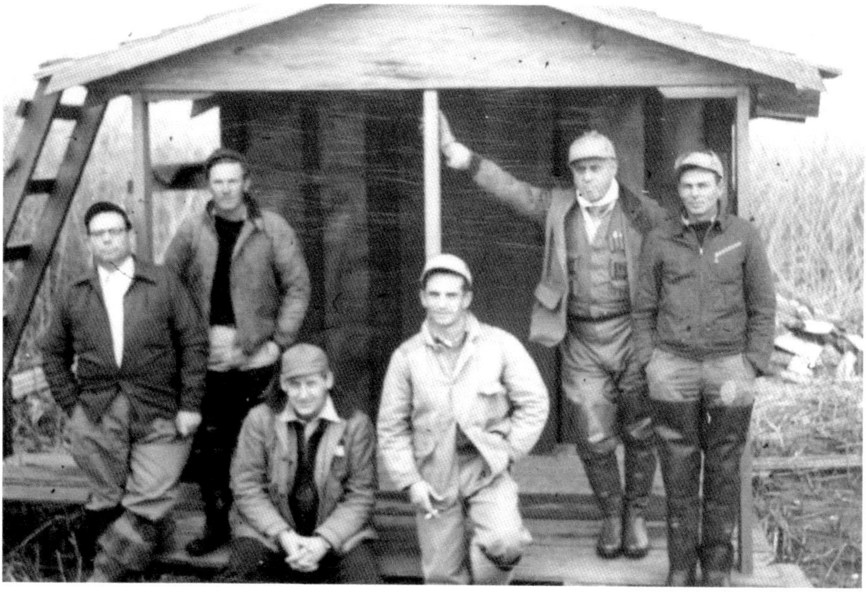

*Left to right:* Orville Woodhouse, Ray Brown, Roy Wilder, Melvin Dowdy, Ben Rodney and St. Clair Saunders at the Marsh Guard Camp. *Courtesy of Larry Woodhouse.*

Dan Leary and J.T. Grandy on opposite sides of the road in Grandy. Larry still has the check for thirty-two dollars drawn on the Bank of Currituck that was paid. Mr. Woodhouse closed the Grandy store (he'd bought that store out for twelve dollars just to close it) and combined the operation in the Leary store. He also got the postmaster job then, a job he had for forty-two years without ever canceling a stamp, taking a vacation or mailing a letter. Miss Ola did it all. In fact, the people around Grandy thought she was the postmaster! Larry said he remembered they'd stay in the store for hours after it closed if the post office was one penny off, over or under. It was easier to find a dollar than a penny, but it had to be right. That's just the way they were. He kept the store until 1948, when he sold it to Melvin Dowdy, but he kept the post office job. According to Larry, that income kept them going when the farming was bad.

Miss Ola introduced Mr. Orville to duck hunting and what it could do for you. When he was growing up, he had coon hunted and sold the hides. He first leased the Narrows Island marsh for hunting. He later gave that up and leased Burrises and Brant Islands from Currituck Club. Larry said Miss Ola was a good shot. She hunted with a 20-gauge double-barrel shotgun.

At this point, I think it is necessary for me to tell you a little about Narrows Island Club since Miss Ola's family was associated with it and I have a lot of pictures of people who worked there. I wrote the history of the club for

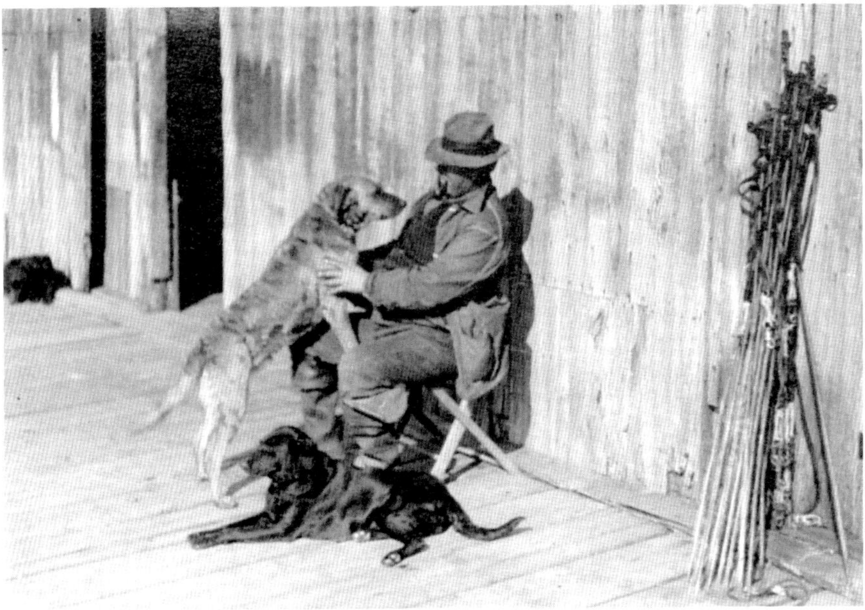

Sportsman at Narrows Island Club. The stakes propped up on the building are stuck down in the water, and live goose decoys are tied to them. *Courtesy of Larry Woodhouse.*

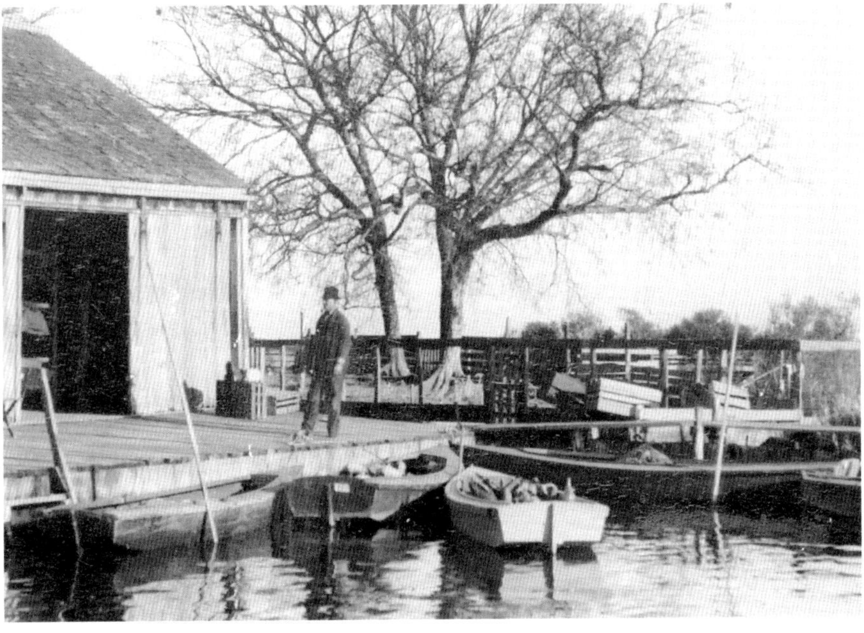

Narrows Island dock. Note the skiffloads of decoys. The skiffs were tucked up in the stern, which meant they towed and poled better. This was before outboard motors. Also note the crates for live decoys. *Courtesy of Larry Woodhouse.*

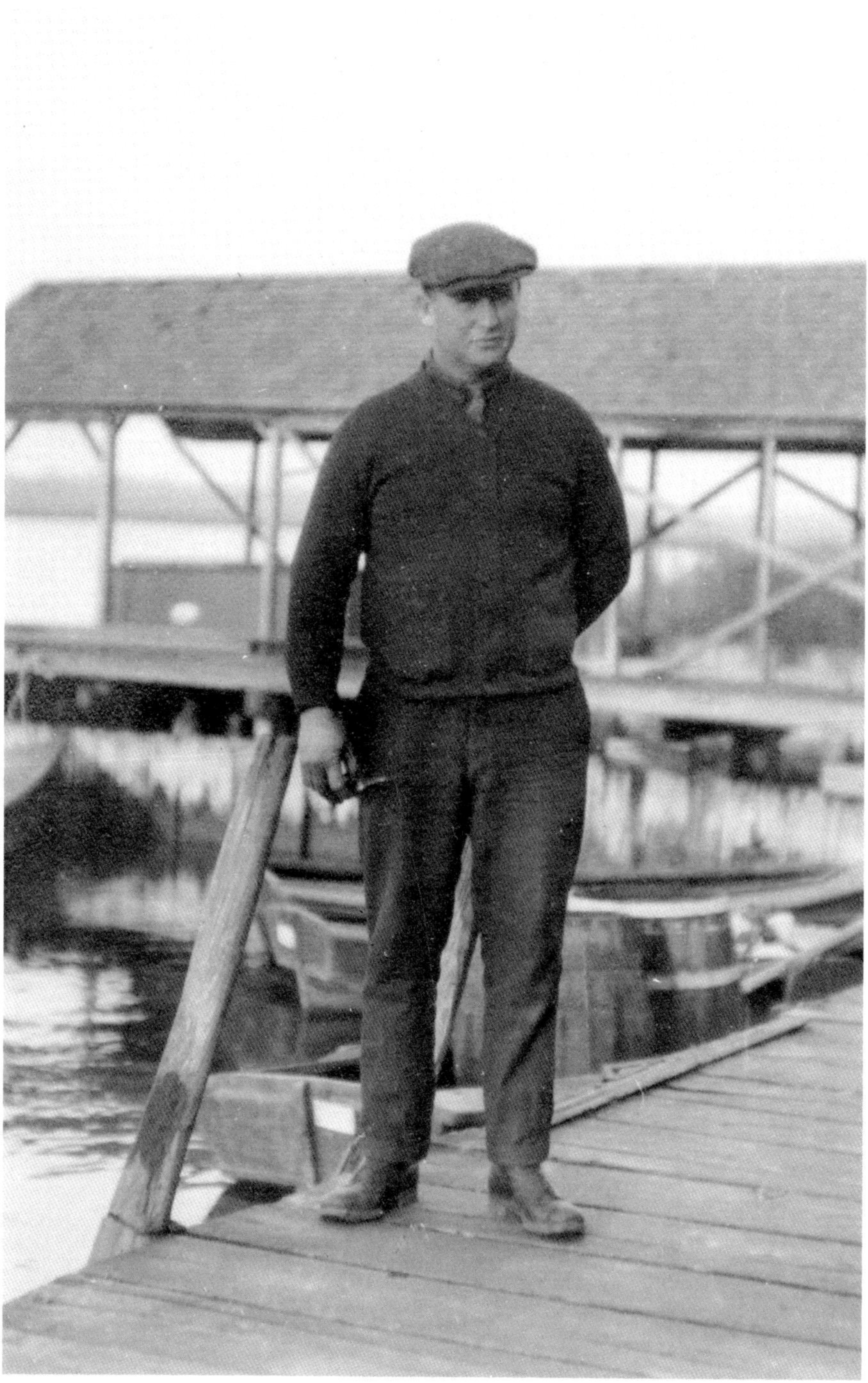

Cleveland Aydlett, superintendent of Narrows Island Club. *Courtesy of Larry Woodhouse.*

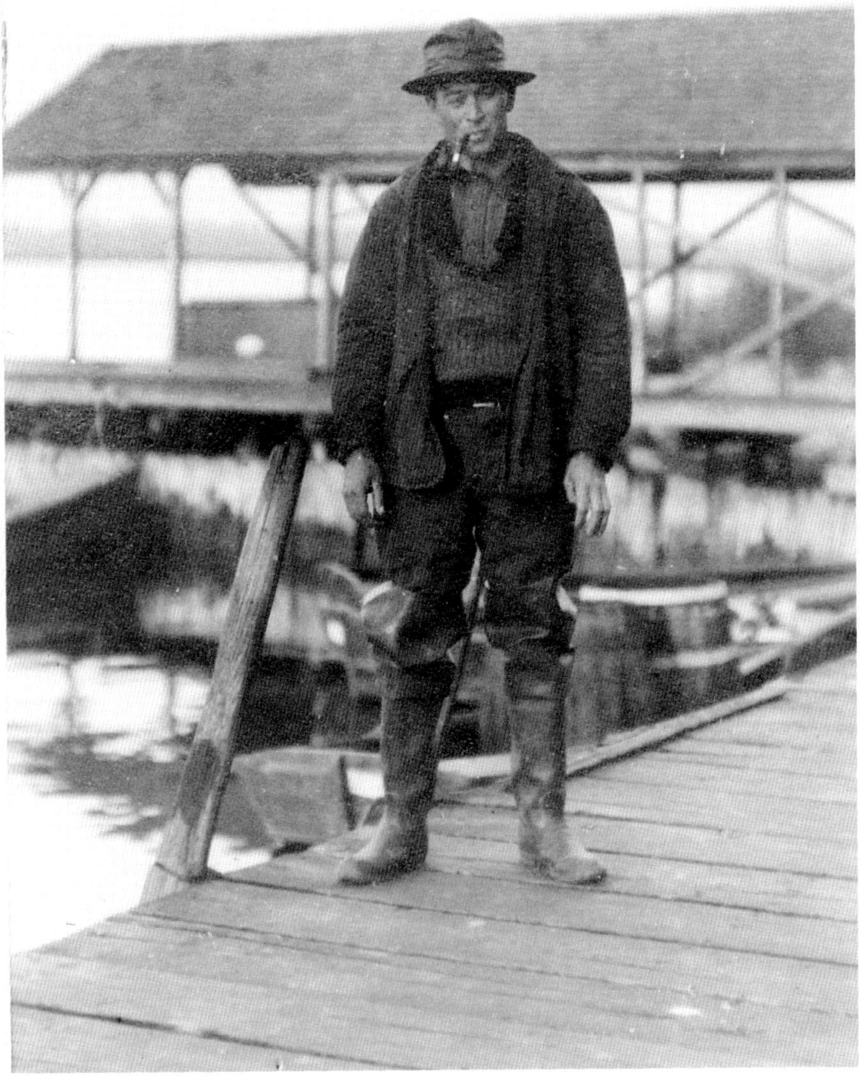

Ike Aydlett guided at Narrows Island Club. He was the father of Miss Ola Woodhouse. *Courtesy of Larry Woodhouse.*

the Currituck County Historical Society in 1976, but I will just touch on it here. The club was organized by a group of men from New York on July 22, 1881. William Rockefeller was one of the later members.

John T. White, who was Carl P. White's daddy, was superintendent of Narrows Island Club from 1910 until he resigned in 1923. At that time, Mr. Cleveland Aydlett was appointed superintendent. He was Miss Ola's uncle. Her daddy, Ike Aydlett, worked there, as did her uncles Mark and John.

Larry Woodhouse told me that Mr. Carl White said that when he was a young boy, Mr. Cleveland Aydlett kinda' took him under his wing and taught him how to manage ducks. He said Mr. Cleveland could bring ducks in your living room with corn. Mr. Carl was the best manager of ducks that I personally have ever known. He was respected by all the old clubs for his ability to manage duck hunting clubs and ducks. He was superintendent of Pine Island Club for thirty-eight years. He was also superintendent of Narrows Island Club from the time Mr. Earl Slick bought it, in 1968, until Mr. Carl died in 1975. At that time, Ernest Brickhouse was appointed superintendent. Ernest held this position until he retired in 1995. At that time, Jeff Davenport got Ernest's job. Andy Newbern is the caretaker at Narrows Island.

Currituck politics has been divided into two factions since before I can remember. One camp was pro–Joseph Knapp and the other was pro–Representative Ed Johnson. When Joseph Knapp bought Mackey Island and moved here in 1918, Representative Johnson—"Boss Hog" of Currituck—had started a Game Commission in Currituck. Regulations charged more for out-of-state hunters than for locals. When Mr. Knapp was out hunting shortly after moving here, the game warden, Norman Balance, went to get him. Mr. Knapp wanted to know what the problem was.

"I'm getting you for two reasons: Ed Johnson wants to meet you and you don't have a local license."

Mr. Knapp argued that he had sent a letter of intent to Clerk of Court Baxter Bell, and he certainly was hunting as a local. Baxter Bell had been appointed by Ed Johnson and, being loyal to him, wouldn't acknowledge the letter. Mr. Knapp said to the sheriff, Bob Flora: "Sheriff, I guess I'm your man." The sheriff evidently saw through it and didn't arrest him; at least, there is no record of it. He was a friend to Mr. Knapp.

There again, it all started over duck-hunting rights and spilled over into the schools. Regarding the schools, the Ed Johnson faction thought Mr. Knapp had too much power over the schools. In 1932, he gave Currituck County more than the citizens of the county paid in ad valorem taxes, mostly to the schools. You can read more about him in my second book, *Currituck Memories and Adventures: More Tales from a Native Gunner.*

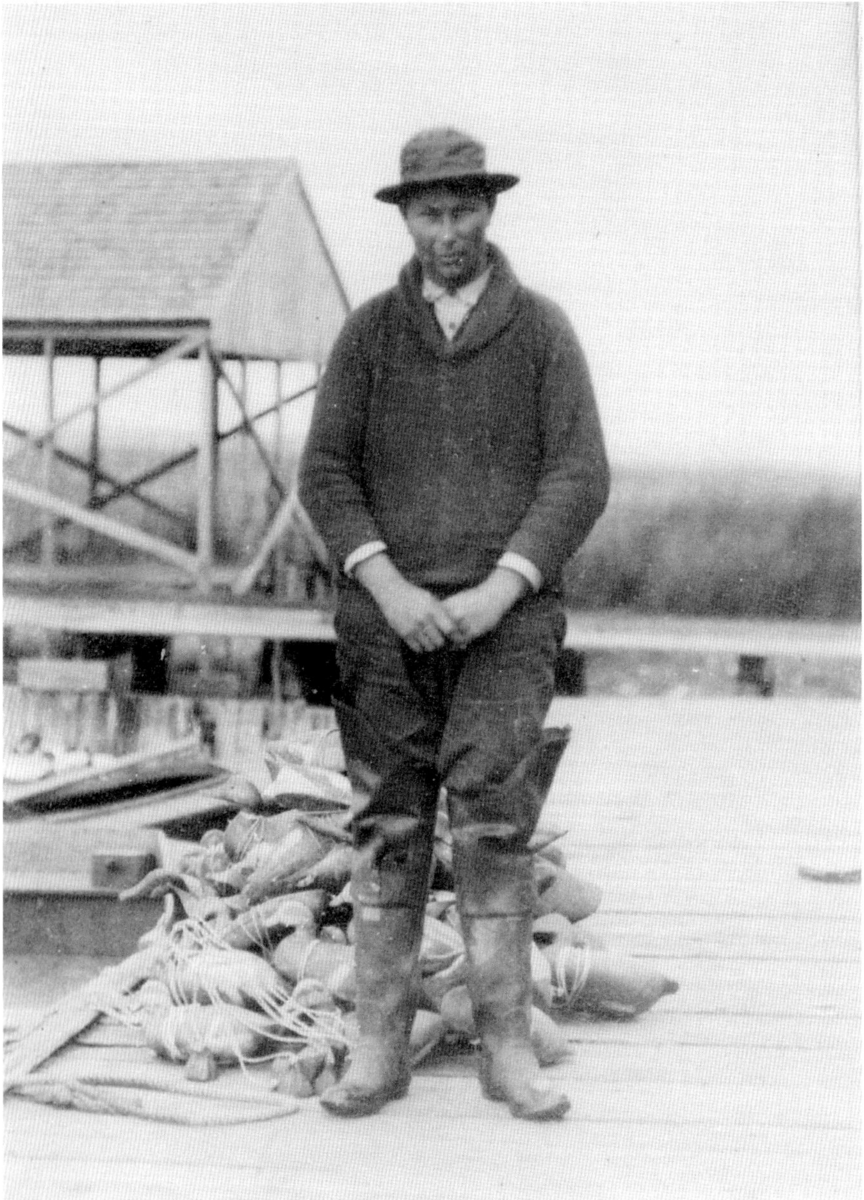

Alphonso Lane worked at Narrows Island Club. He was one of the head carpenters who built the Whalehead Club. He was one of the best-known carpenters in Currituck. He built many houses on the mainland of Currituck. He was later employed, for twenty years, by Mr. William S. Gray from Greenwich, Connecticut, who owned Bells Island Club. Mr. Lane's daughter, Edna, was my Daddy's first secretary when he started practicing law in Currituck in 1926 and stayed with him until he became a Superior Court judge in 1946. She then ran for and was elected the first female Currituck County register of deeds. *Courtesy of Larry Woodhouse.*

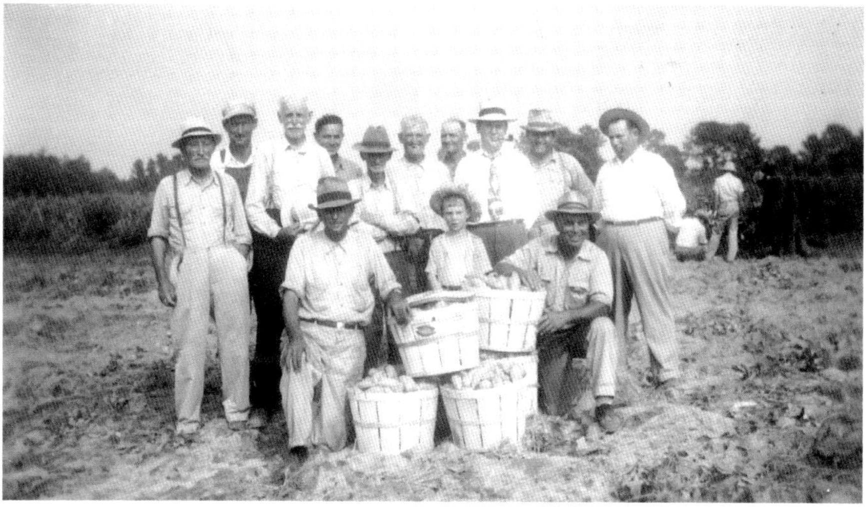

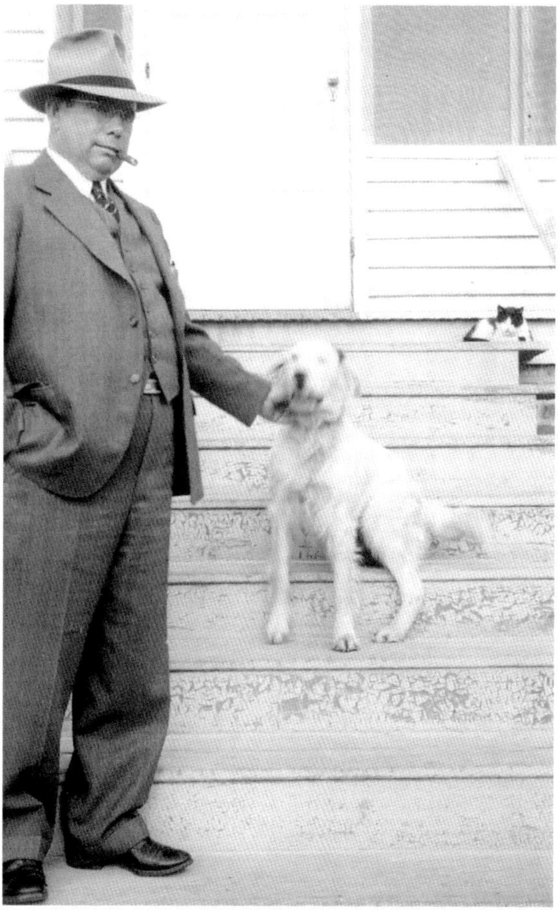

*Above:* Sweet potatoes and workers in field. Woodhouse is on the far right. *Courtesy of Larry Woodhouse.*

*Left:* Orville Woodhouse and his bird dog Mack. Larry said his daddy would leave Mack in the field with the field hands. One day, he told somebody he really had a good crew of field hands: they were all working when he went in the field. Somebody told him the reason for that was Mack started barking when he heard the truck coming. *Courtesy of Larry Woodhouse.*

Mr. Orville was an original member of the pro-Knapp faction. Mr. Knapp established the Currituck Mutual Exchange in the Depression years to help farmers with loans and to give them some buying and selling power as a group. During these years, Mr. Woodhouse was the Mutual Exchange representative for the southern end of the county. When the exchange went out of business in 1935, he opened his produce warehouse. While everyone knew he was a Knapp man, he also had the respect of the other faction. With factions being what they were, that said a lot for Mr. Orville's talent as a politician.

Mr. Orville wound up having the second biggest produce warehouse in eastern North Carolina, second only to Scott and Halstead in Weeksville. He contracted Irish potatoes and green beans with farmers in Camden, Pasquotank and Currituck Counties. Mr. Orville was the pioneer in North Carolina in installing a potato grader that would wash and dry potatoes as well as grade them and put them in five-and-ten paper, and fifty- and one-hundred-pound burlap bags. This cut out the middleman and he could send them straight to A&P, Safeway and other chain grocery stores.

In Raleigh, Mr. Orville Woodhouse was known as the "Duke of Currituck." In Currituck, he was known as "Long Coat." He wore an overcoat from fall through the middle of May, when there was no more threat of frost. He said he didn't mind "such jocular titles." His grandfather, Major Woodhouse, was the sergeant-at-arms of the House of Representatives in the 1920s and was known as the "Hell raiser from Currituck." Larry said he never knew him, but Miss Kate Tillett said he took after him. Mr. Orville said of Larry, "He thinks if you're not living on the edge, you're wasting space on this earth."

The following are stories as his son, Larry Woodhouse, told me.

# Inspiring Change Through Challenge

Mr. Orville Woodhouse was elected as chairman of the Currituck County Board of Education in 1944. At that time, Frank Aycock was the superintendent of schools. Frank Aycock told Larry that Mr. Orville was the cause of him becoming a lawyer. He said he used to go and sit on the front porch and talk with Mr. Orville on Sunday mornings. One Sunday, he went up there and was drunk. The conversation went something like this:

Mr. Orville said, "Frank, I'm going to fire you."

"Orville, even though you're chairman, under the law you can't fire me."

"No, but we can hold your check up."

"That's just as good as firing me. I have a wife and three kids to support."

Frank Aycock said he went to law school after that to see if Orville Woodhouse really could fire him.

I personally remember when Mr. Aycock was superintendent of schools here and I remember when he went to law school. My daddy was a lawyer and, for the last twenty-six years of his career, a Superior Court judge. I can remember Mr. Aycock spending many hours at our house talking to Daddy.

I also remember people saying that, during World War II, Frank Aycock invented the sight on the Springfield rifle.

# World's Most Creative Name-Dropper

In 1949, Kerr Scott was elected governor of North Carolina and, of course, there were many appointments that had to be made. The Wildlife Commission was two years old at the time. There were nine members and holding a seat there was a very prestigious position. There was a big fight for the appointment.

A bunch of politicians were invited to a watermelon cutting at the home of Governor Scott at Haw River. At the time, Mr. Ray Midgett was clerk of court here. He got the Currituck County commissioners and commissioners from several other counties to endorse Orville Woodhouse for the Wildlife Commission appointment. There was a big delegation that went to the watermelon cutting: Ray Midgett, Howard Sumrell, Jim Taylor and many more.

There was also a man there named Elmer Dowdy who was a friend and supporter of the governor. He had grown up in Currituck and had gone to school with Orville and Ola Woodhouse, but had moved to Hillsborough to teach.

There were so many people at the party that Elmer Dowdy couldn't get the attention of the governor to put the word in for Orville. That didn't stop him from doing what he set out to do. He went in the house and into the governor's bathroom and wrote on a roll of toilet paper: "Orville Woodhouse—Grandy, NC—Wildlife Commission—1st District." Then he got a piece of paper off the governor's desk, wrote the same thing on it and pinned it to the governor's bed. This is a true story!

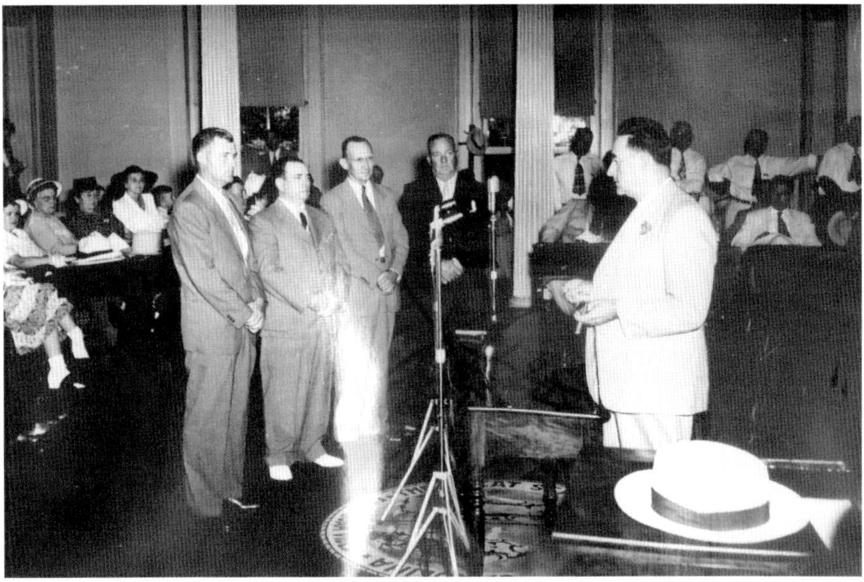

Orville Woodhouse being sworn in to the North Carolina Wildlife Commission in 1949. *Courtesy of Larry Woodhouse.*

Mr. Woodhouse didn't know all this, but he got the appointment, and later the Scotts got to be good friends with the Woodhouses. The governor started coming to Currituck to go duck hunting. He was here one time and they were talking about Elmer Dowdy.

"Yes, he's a good friend and supporter," the governor said. "Orville, did you know he wrote you up on a piece of toilet paper one time?"

"Do what?" Orville asked.

The governor told him the story and then said he had no choice but to appoint him. He said his wife said, "I'm scared to open my underwear drawer. I don't know what's going to be in there. Appoint this man, don't Elmer Dowdy is going to take over our whole life!"

# Consider Yourself Warned

Bud Lupton was a hunting guide. He got caught selling geese after the season to a federal undercover agent. The agent carried him down to try him in court and put him before Judge Larkin.

Judge Larkin came to Currituck a lot to duck hunt and always stayed at Dorothy and Colon Grandy's, and Bud Lupton was his guide. When the case came up, Judge Larkin said, "Bud, it's generally known that you are my guide and I'd feel better and I know you would if we get another judge to come in here and try you."

"Oh, no, no, Judge. I'd just as soon be tried by you as anybody and whatever it is, it is." The judge agreed and the trial started.

They put the evidence on and Judge Larkin said, "Okay, Bud, I have no choice but to find you guilty and I'm going to fine you $100." Larry said Bud just sat back and grinned. Then Judge Larkin turned around and said, "per goose."

Bud hollered, "You son of a bitch!"

The man who told Larry this was a bailiff or U.S. marshal at the time. He told Larry it was the funniest thing he'd ever seen in the courtroom.

# Club Power

Terry Sanford was Kerr Scott's campaign manager when Scott ran for the Senate. Mr. Orville had been friends with Kerr Scott when he was secretary of agriculture. When Sanford got to be governor, Larry said he was here all the time. In fact, they called room 5 at Walnut Island "the Governor's Room."

Ducks played a big part in politics in the Sanford administration. There was a group that was left over from the Scott days and they were called the Branch Head Boys. Larry said there was a plug of tobacco somewhere around there that had that name on it. If you were a real, genuine Branch Head Boy, you had to have a plug of that tobacco. It was apple tobacco that Kerr Scott chewed.

Judge John Larkin had been chairman of the Democratic Party. He ran for governor against I. Beverly Lake, Sanford and some others. On one of his trips to Raleigh, Mr. Woodhouse told Sanford they had to do something for John Larkin. Sanford tensed at the suggestion about his old opponent and sarcastically said, "What do you want me to do, make him a federal judge?"

"How did you guess?" Mr. Orville replied. "That's exactly what this little group of people want you to do for him."

"You're kidding!"

"I'm not kidding. John Larkin would make a wonderful federal judge. All you have to do is call Kennedy." Sanford had been the first person

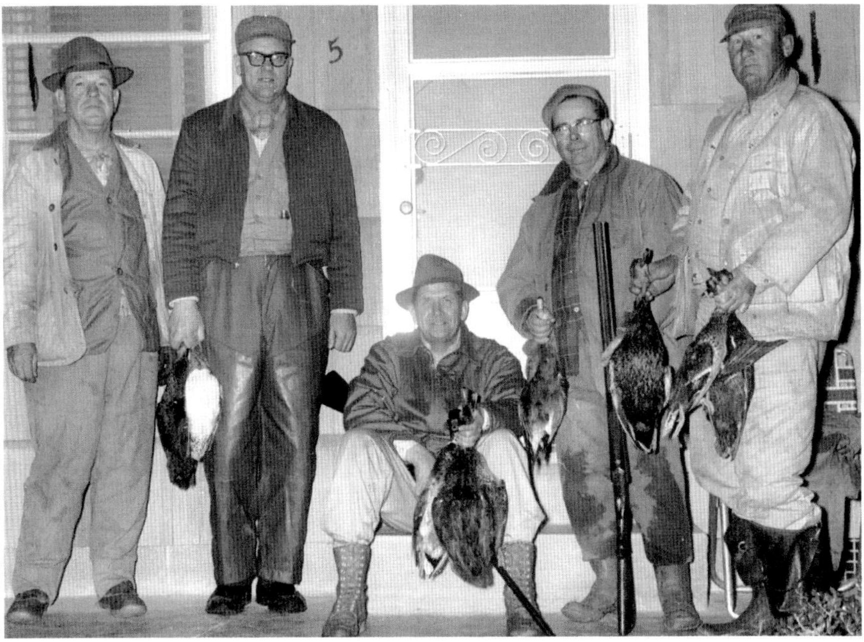

*Left to right:* S.J. Farris, the first owner of Walnut Island Motel; Melvin Hern, in charge of Farmers Home Administration for North Carolina; Governor Sanford; Orville Woodhouse; and Altas Outlaw. *Courtesy of Larry Woodhouse.*

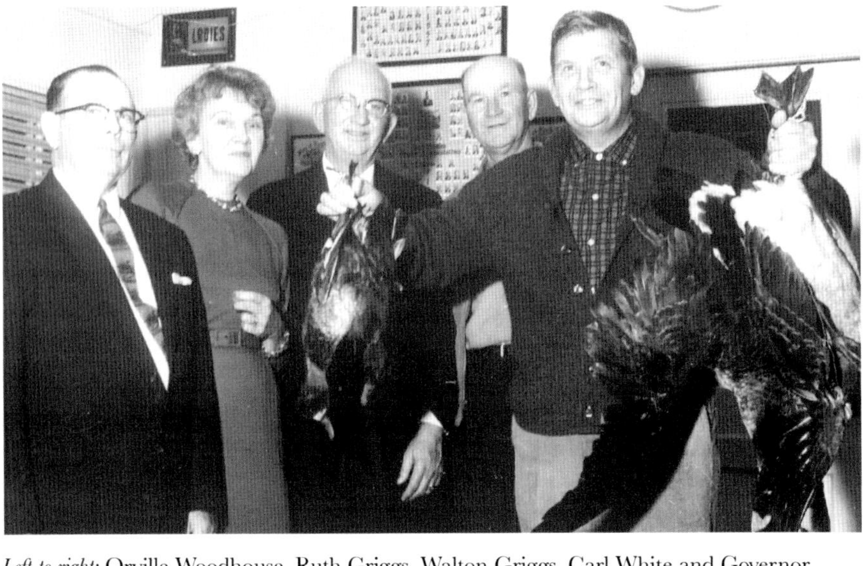

*Left to right:* Orville Woodhouse, Ruth Griggs, Walton Griggs, Carl White and Governor Sanford. Walton and Ruth Griggs owned and operated the Point Harbor Grill. Walton Griggs was also in the North Carolina House of Representatives for many years. Carl White was superintendent of Pine Island Club for thirty-eight years. *Courtesy of Larry Woodhouse.*

from North Carolina to nominate Kennedy for president. The call was made and John Larkin got his position as federal judge.

President Kennedy invited Governor Sanford to the Liberty Bowl football game in Philadelphia. While there, Sanford invited President Kennedy to come duck hunting in Currituck. He accepted right away. The president's hunting trip with Orville Woodhouse and Terry Sanford was planned. They were to stay at Pine Island Club. Security had already gone out to check the area out and the trip was OK'd. The president was assassinated just before he was to come to Currituck on that hunting trip.

# Coon Hunting

Terry Sanford had Governor Endicott Peabody and his wife come to Currituck to duck hunt with Woodhouse. Larry and Mr. Orville carried him to Piluntary Pond, and they were shooting blackheads and Peabody wouldn't quit shooting. He had never been duck hunting before, but he said that was the most fun he'd ever had in his life. They had to walk in there to hunt, and when Larry and Governor Sanford were walking out, Larry told the governor, "He don't want to come. He's having too good a time."

"You go back and tell him if he don't want to spend the night out here he better come on because we're going." When Larry went back in and told Governor Peabody, he said, "To hell with him. I'm having fun." Larry told him they really did need to get out of there or there wouldn't be any ducks out there the next day. Peabody finally agreed.

Back at home, Mr. Orville said, "If they want to hunt so bad, we're going to carry them coon hunting tonight."

Larry said they carried them over behind the Willy Leary field. The dogs treed a coon and they were walking through the woods to get to the tree when a limb smacked Sanford in the face. He told Larry to tell his daddy when they got back home that coon hunting went out with Daniel Boone. "Don't worry about us hunting coon anymore. We'll stick with duck hunting."

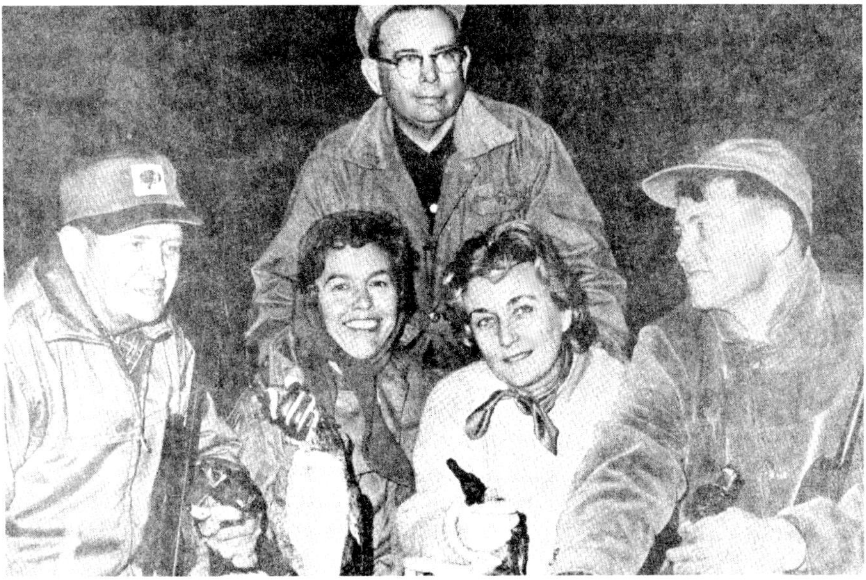

*Left to right:* Governor Terry Sanford, his wife Margaret, Mrs. Endicott Peabody and Governor Peabody of Massachusetts. Orville Woodhouse is standing behind them. *Courtesy of Larry Woodhouse.*

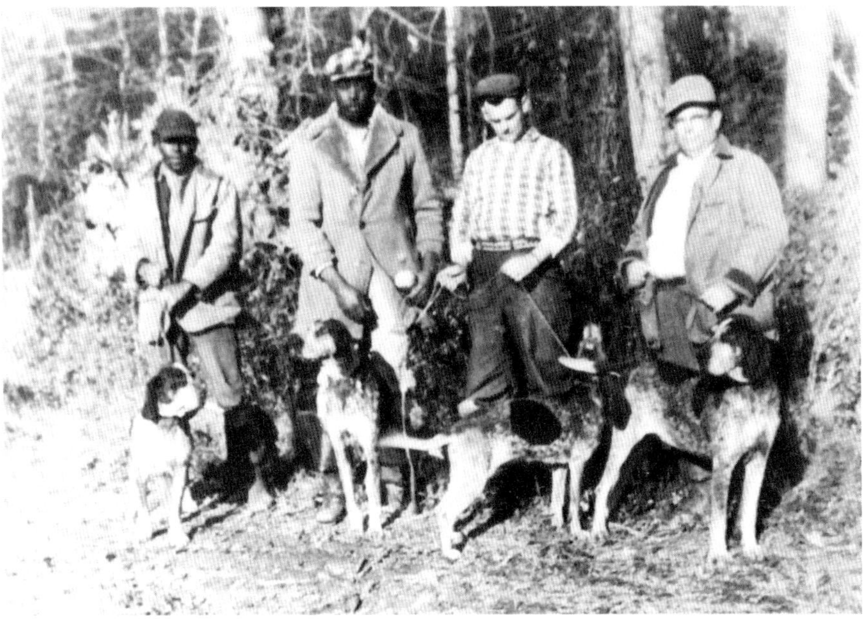

*Left to right:* Howard Jones, Roosevelt Lee, Larry Woodhouse and Orville Woodhouse. *Courtesy of Larry Woodhouse.*

# Talking Dogs with President Johnson

Mr. Woodhouse got an award as Wildlife Conservationist of the State. He got an invitation to go to Washington to shake hands with President Johnson. Governor Sanford told Larry that there were about two thousand people there to shake hands with President Johnson about some kind of conservation deal. He said the line was going right along until Mr. Woodhouse got there and the line stopped moving. Finally, security went up there to see what was going on. President Johnson said, "Just a damn minute. I'm talking to this man." On the way back home, Sanford asked Mr. Woodhouse what he'd been talking about with the president.

"We were talking about dogs," Mr. Woodhouse said. "The president had bluetick hounds one time and we got in a conversation about dogs. When security came up, the president said 'Let 'em wait. I'm talking to this man about dogs.'"

"I'm glad to hear that," Governor Sanford replied. "I thought you had some national secrets going."

Larry has a pen the president gave his father with the president's name on it.

# Eatin' Crow for Breakfast

Mr. Clyde Patten was executive director of the North Carolina Wildlife Commission. Larry said one of the most historical things his daddy ever got involved in was the firing of Clyde Patten. Mr. Orville told Larry they would have these meetings with all these people and if Mr. Patten didn't want to hear it he'd cut his hearing aid down; half the time they'd ask him something and he didn't even know what they were talking about. One day, seven of the commission members got together and said, "Clyde has been here long enough. We're gonna' fix this." Mr. Woodhouse being chairman, he had him fired.

"After that I could have been killed in a car wreck and the phone wouldn't have rung as many times as it did then," Larry said his father said. For three days and nights, calls came in from the Wildlife Federation members, the Chathams, the Haneses and more. The newspaper reporters were flying and driving down here saying, "Oh, you've got to do this" or "You've got to do that."

Larry said they were at the breakfast table when the phone rang and his daddy got up to answer it in the other room. When he came back, Miss Ola asked, "What was that about?"

"You know what that was about. Woodrow Price with the *News and Observer* about Clyde Patten." Larry said his mama looked at his daddy and said, "You had enough clout to fire Clyde Patten?"

"That's right."

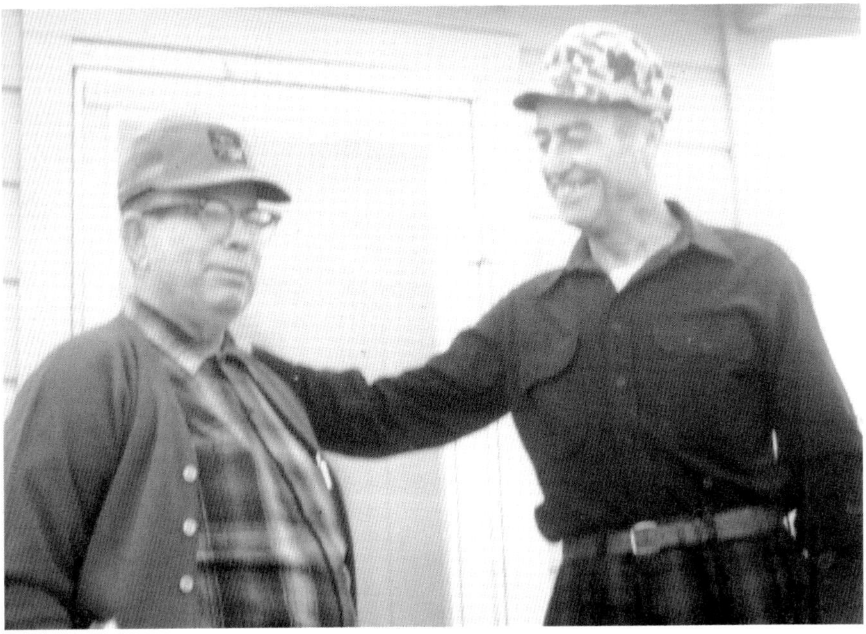

Orville Woodhouse (left) and Senator Tom White from Kinston. The request: "Reinstate Clyde Patten." *Courtesy of Larry Woodhouse.*

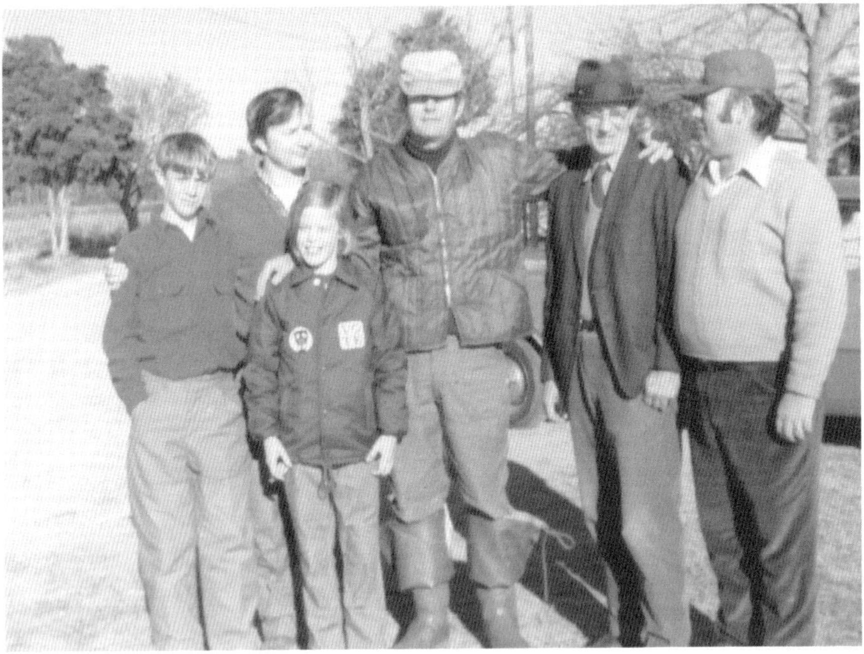

*Left to right:* Governor Jim Hunt's children (he is standing behind them), Gillam Wood, Governor Hunt's father and Larry Woodhouse. *Courtesy of Larry Woodhouse.*

"Have you got enough clout to reinstate him?"

"What?"

"You heard me," she said, "I said do you have enough political clout to reinstate Clyde Patten?"

Mr. Woodhouse looked at Larry and said, "Crow comes in many flavors, even at breakfast."

"I reckon it does."

That day, Larry was to take Tom White—Senate pro tem—duck hunting out on the North River. His daddy told him to tell Tom White he wanted to see him before he left for home in Kinston. When Larry told Mr. White that, he said, "I ain't sure I want to see Orville."

"Why's that?" Larry wanted to know.

"He's in the hot seat. Don't get me in it." Larry told him about the conversation at breakfast and said he thought his daddy wanted Mr. White to help him construct a letter that would reinstate Mr. Patten and not make him look so bad. Mr. White said, "Well, I'm your man. I'll stop and talk to him."

Ducks figured into the reinstatement when Mr. Orville invited Mr. Patten to hunt in Currituck. Mr. Patten got ready to go out hunting in a black suit and tie. Miss Ola said, "Lord, have mercy, that shows you what Clyde Patten knows about hunting." Mr. Woodhouse just answered that she needn't worry; he'd take care of him.

Larry and his father took Mr. Patten and a guest hunting in Piluntery Pond and Mr. Patten couldn't hit a thing. Finally, Mr. Woodhouse got kind of behind the blind enough so that he could shoot at the very same time that Mr. Patten shot. The ducks started falling. Mr. Woodhouse would say, "Clyde, that was a good shot." Mr. Patten would clear his throat and say, "Well, ah, if I do say so myself, it wasn't a bad shot." Mr. Woodhouse didn't want the ducks scared to death with the banging. He wanted to get their limit and get out of there.

Needless to say, Mr. Clyde Patten was reinstated as executive director of the North Carolina Wildlife Commission.

Governor Jim Hunt is not featured in any of these stories, but he did come to Currituck to hunt with Orville Woodhouse and I felt I should include this picture of him and his family.

# High Dollar Cabbage

Mr. Woodhouse sent Ernest Orville Beasley to New York with a ten-wheeler load of cabbage. Ernest turned the truck over in the mouth of the Holland Tunnel in Jersey City, New Jersey, and cabbages were strewed from one end to the other. New Jersey sent Mr. Woodhouse a bill for the cleanup that was for more than their whole farm was worth. Orville called the mayor and somehow got the bill down to about $700, which

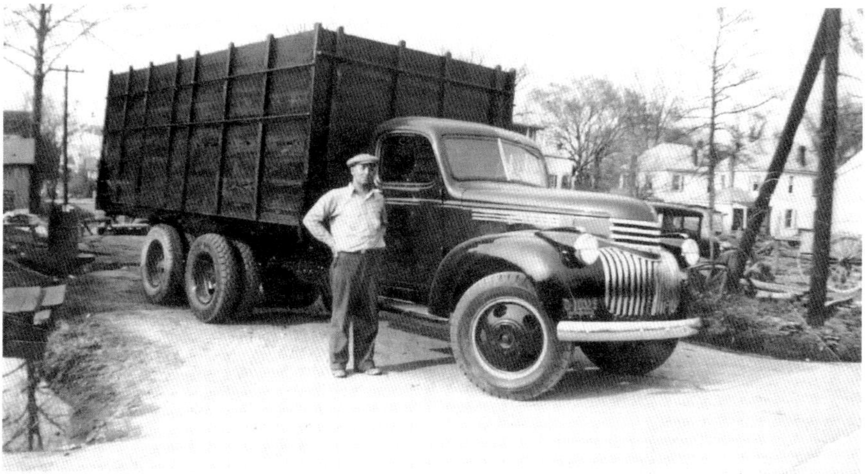

Eddie Dowdy's 1945 ten-wheeler. *Courtesy of Larry Woodhouse.*

was still a lot in those days. Miss Ola said, "Don't ever send Ernest Orville Beasley anywhere."

Not long after that, Buck Hall, just out of school, was anxious to drive a truck. Junior Baum had a 1951 Ford cab-over F-600 and a short, single-axle open-top trailer. It was short enough to get on the Washington Street market in New York. This was Buck's first trip. When he went around the curve on the Northwest Bridge, the rotten right side of the old trailer gave way, dumping cabbage in the Northwest River. When Miss Ola heard about it, she said, "My God, I hope Chesapeake don't send us a bill like New Jersey did."

Buck told me he limped on up to Mr. Bill Forehand's and they loaded the cabbage that was left on another truck.

Buck Hall went on to make a career out of truck driving. I bought a new 1961 B-61 Mack for him to drive and then later we owned several trucks together. You can read more about him in my last book, *Currituck Memories and Adventures.*

# Telling the Swan Truth

Governor Luther Hodges called Mr. Woodhouse and wanted to have a wild dinner for some folks from out of state. Mr. Woodhouse told Larry to get eight geese for him. He and Ralph Sears went out and couldn't find any geese, so they killed eight swans and had them dressed. This was before it was legal to kill swans. The fine was $500 each. They put the dressed swans in a box and Mr. Woodhouse got Scott Sawyer, a game warden, to take them to Edenton. Then another game warden picked them up and relayed them on to the next game warden's territory. It went on this way until they got to Raleigh.

The governor wrote this nice letter about how good those geese were. Larry said he and Ralph couldn't stand it. They told Scott Sawyer, "Do you know what you were hauling?"

"What?"

"We killed eight swans. You were hauling swan!"

"You all are lying." Everybody said those boys ought not to be lying like that. Larry said, "They ate a $4,000 dinner and didn't even know it."

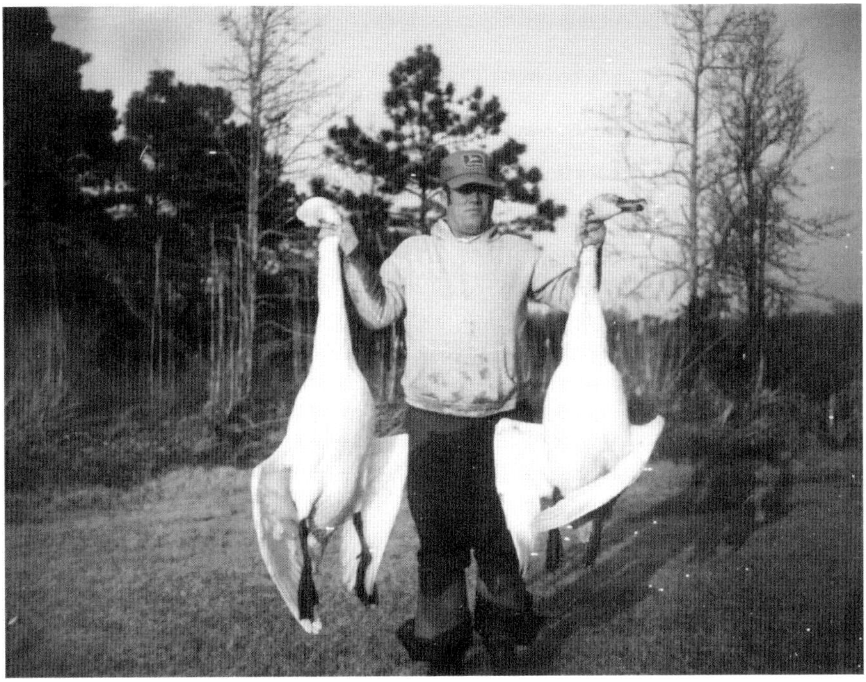

Ralph Sears with the swans that were sent to Governor Hodges as geese. *Courtesy of Larry Woodhouse.*

# Keeping a Secret "'Til Death Do Us Part"

Ralph Saunders was clerk of court in Currituck, and Victor Zinc was Larry Woodhouse's brother-in-law and was in the Coast Guard. In fact, he headed up the rifle and pistol team. Both men were expert shots. According to Larry, they just didn't miss. Period.

Those two men and Larry were in a duck blind, hunting. Things were about half froze up and the ducks were flying. Larry said they had him sitting in the middle. Along came a swan and Ralph Saunders shot him. It hit the water and looked like a bedsheet spread out there. They looked up and here come that federal helicopter hovering right over them and picked up the swan. Larry hadn't even fired his gun and was glad he hadn't. The helicopter landed onshore and when the agents got out, they had all their credentials. Larry knew the guy flying: Al Doteman. One other fellow was with him. According to Larry, they were after them all the time. They were really after his daddy, but he had quit duck hunting and had gone back to just coon hunting.

They told the warden they hadn't been out there long and the swan was there when they got there. They said there were a lot of people firelighting around there. The big guy told Larry, "Come here and stick your finger right here." He was pointing to its butt and Larry did as he was told.

"You feel how warm that is? That swan ain't been dead very long."

"He sure hasn't, but we ain't been out here very long."

They got home about 5:00 p.m. Ralph Saunders said, "Don't you all ever breathe a word of this. I'm clerk of court."

"Yeah," Victor agreed, "and I'd get kicked out of the military."

"I ain't got to worry," Larry said. "I ain't fired my gun." They told him not to let his daddy know because they didn't know if they'd be arrested or not. Just stick to the story.

Larry's family was sitting down eating dinner when the phone rang. His daddy got up and answered it, then came back and asked Larry, "Did you all have company in the duck blind today?"

"Yes'r."

"That was the *News and Observer* calling wanting to know if I had a comment."

"Comment about what?"

"Well, I guess your license has an 'L' on it and they thought it was me. If you ever have a child, don't name him after yourself. Now you just well tell me what's up."

Larry stuck to the story. The swan was there when they got there. Mr. Woodhouse said, "Warren Lupton [he was lead federal game warden] and those two men will be in my office at 9:00 a.m. Monday. I want you, Victor and Ralph to be there."

Warren Lupton and Mr. Woodhouse were good friends, but the other two weren't so easy to get along with. When they all got there, they sent Larry and Victor out of the room and sat Ralph Saunders down in the room with them. They said, "Now, Mr. Saunders, you are clerk of court. You're an officer of the law. Who killed that swan?" Ralph stuck to the story.

Larry told me that Ralph said he could tell the story after he'd died, but to stick to the story until then. With both Ralph and Victor gone, Larry felt it was all right to tell the story as it happened. He said, "It's a good story now, but it weren't so good then."

# Costly Liquor

Wallace Smith was the president of the Bank of Currituck. You would have to have known him as I knew him to fully appreciate this statement, but he and his wife, Miss Rena, *were* the Bank of Currituck. Nobody else worked there. They had no children, just a cat named "Bunkie." When the Bank of Currituck built that big new bank at Moyock with a cupola on top, I said, "Tommy Moore [president of the bank now] must be putting that up there as a memorial to Bunkie."

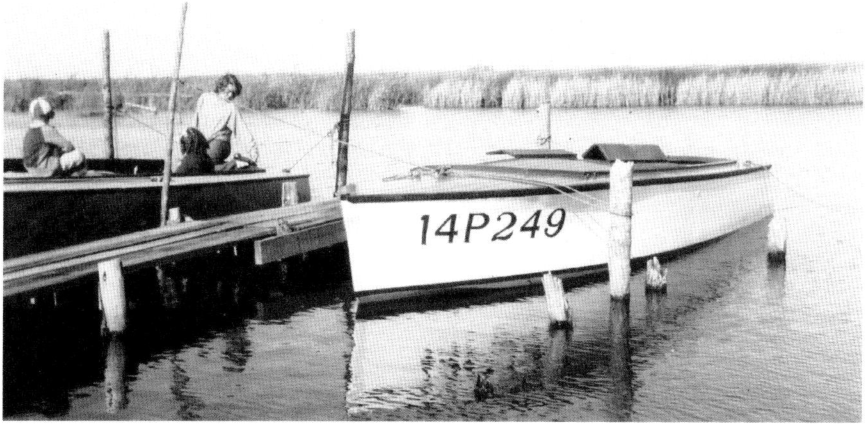


The *Phyllis Rae* at dock in Neal's Creek. *Courtesy of Larry Woodhouse.*

Mr. Smith loved his liquor. He'd drink every evening as soon as the bank closed, but he didn't drink during banking hours. Miss Rena saw to that.

Larry told me that Mr. Smith had heard about this fast boat Orville Woodhouse had and he wanted to ride in her. On the appointed afternoon, Mr. Smith went down to Neal's Creek and they got in the boat and were heading down toward the south mouth of the creek with the throttle wide open. The steering cable broke just then and the boat ran up into the marsh, throwing Mr. Smith straight in the marsh. He'd been sitting in the bow. He got up and told Mr. Woodhouse, "I'm going to call every damn note you have in the Bank of Currituck."

"For what? Are you hurt?" Mr. Woodhouse wanted to know.

"No, I'm not hurt. It ain't that. It broke my liquor bottle." He had a pint in his pocket.

# Guarding Against the Warden

When Larry Woodhouse was about ten years old, he was out hunting one day in the Hammocks with Harold Cartwright. His daddy didn't go out with them in the morning, but showed up later in the day. They only got a few ducks after Mr. Orville joined them. Larry and Harold had killed too many ducks already, but they didn't want Mr. Woodhouse to know it so they hid them in the engine box.

Mr. Johnny Guard was a game warden then. When they started to leave to go home, Mr. Guard came and started to get in the boat with them.

Harold wouldn't let him get in the boat. Johnny said, "I'm going to get in that boat." Harold said, "I'll take this shoving oar and I'll guarantee you ain't getting in this boat!"

Mr. Woodhouse didn't say much, but when they got back to Neal's Creek landing, he said, "What's going on with you and Johnny Guard to not let him in the boat?"

"Larry killed too many ducks."

"What do you mean he killed too many ducks?" Mr. Woodhouse asked. Harold lifted the lid to the engine box and showed him it was half full of ducks. Mr. Woodhouse told Larry, "Son, you're going to have to hunt with your grandfather or somebody else. You are not going to hunt in the boat with me." Larry said he didn't think he hunted over three times in the same boat with his daddy after that.

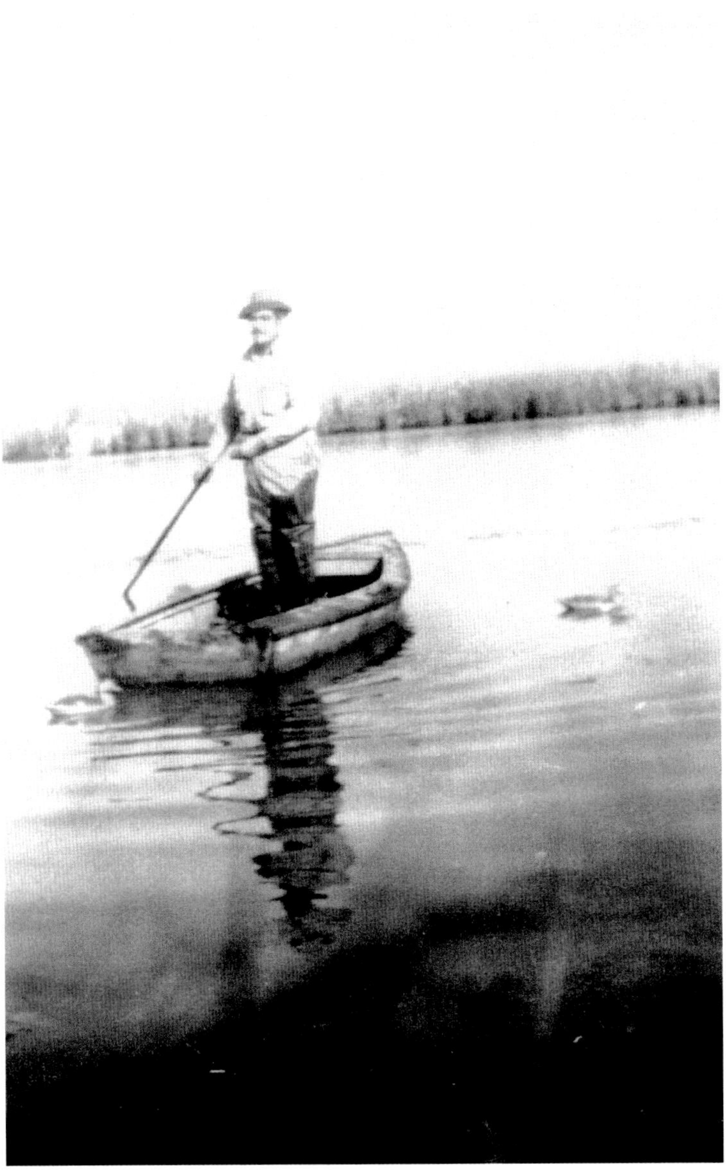

Bruce Smith in a pond on the Narrows Island property in 1948. *Courtesy of Larry Woodhouse.*

# Snap Beans

Miss Ola didn't want Mr. Orville to plant fall snap beans because they were a big gamble. Mr. Woodhouse had a cottage at the beach and sent Miss Ola and the kids to the beach. In about two weeks, they were coming back up and, all of a sudden, Miss Ola said, "Well, what do you think that is growing out there?" Mr. Orville said, "Well, you know the trade wanted me to plant a few." Larry said first thing you know he'd have five hundred acres.

The south end of Currituck is a peninsula; Currituck Sound is on the east and North River on the west. Being this close to the water means it doesn't frost as quick as it does in other places. This means you could have snap beans later in the fall when the prices are higher.

Larry said one time his daddy and Mr. Charlie Wright (Dr. Charles and Caroline Wright's father) had a patch together and they made $10,000. Mr. Charlie said he was going to buy his part up in bird dogs.

Here's a personal example of how much of a gamble snap beans were. The last time I planted any that were not contracted, I had fifteen acres. The day I picked them they were selling for four dollars a bushel. I sent them to Boston and, by the time they got there, they had fallen so low I wouldn't have had enough to pay the freight if they hadn't been on my trucks.

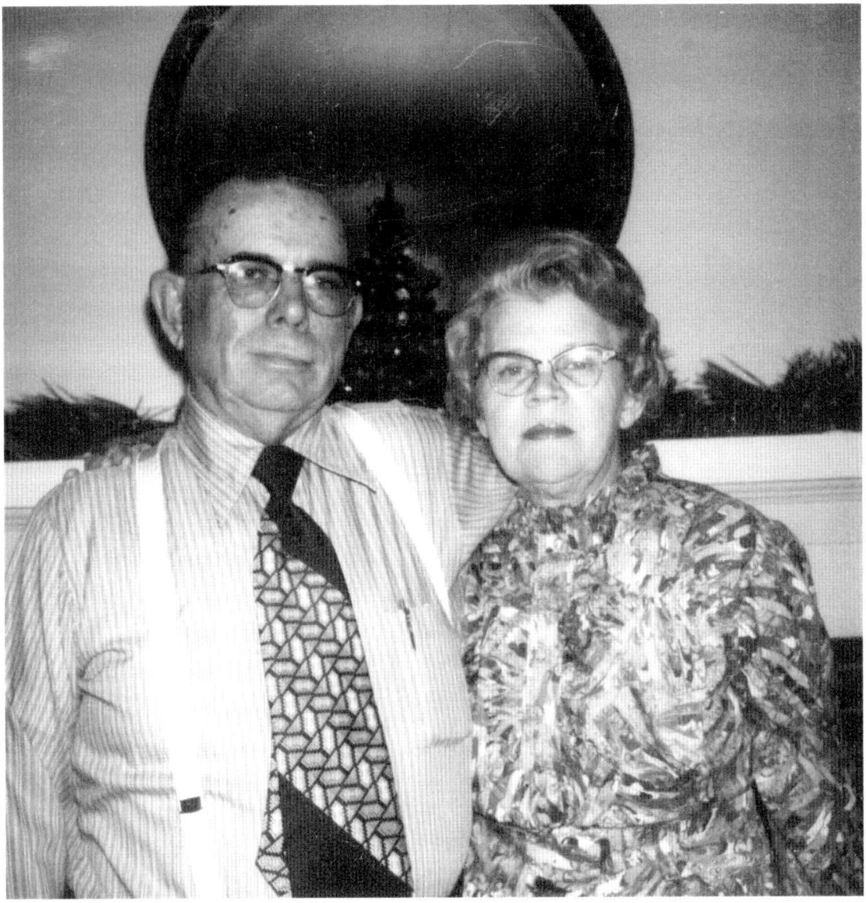

Orville and Ola Woodhouse. *Courtesy of Larry Woodhouse.*

# Irish Potato Blues

In 1956, Mr. Woodhouse sold potatoes for ten dollars per hundred pounds at the packing shed. Miss Ola told Larry they made a million dollars that year. In 1957, he lost that and some more. In that year, it never rained on some of his farms from the day he planted them until the day he dug them. I know this is true because I had some contracted to him that he never dug.

Wilbert Forbes was from Shiloh in Camden County, but he had some political job in Raleigh. I think it was burial commissioner. He had somebody in Camden County looking after his farming operation. This was before Larry Forbes got old enough to farm. He had two hundred acres of potatoes contracted to Mr. Woodhouse at seventy-five dollars an acre.

Larry said Wilbert went home from Raleigh to settle up. He was back there in the back office with Mr. Woodhouse, and Larry and Miss Ola were out in the front office. Larry thought they were laughing, but Wilbert Forbes was crying. He told Mr. Woodhouse that his mother actually owned the land and she didn't know the potatoes were under contract. She was expecting all this money and he was only going home with the contracted $15,000. Mr. Woodhouse said, "My Lord, let me think about it and come back tomorrow."

Miss Ola went back there and said, "What in the world ails Wilbert Forbes?" Mr. Orville told her the story. She said, "Orville, do you believe that story? He didn't cry last year and the year before when *we* didn't make any money." Anyway, he made a deal with Wilbert. He gave him more money and said if he (Woodhouse) lost money the next year, they'd adjust up until it was over with. When the next year came, Wilbert said his mother didn't want to plant any more potatoes.

# Life Lesson

Mr. Charlie Wright was a big produce farmer here and he had a little store. His wife, Miss Mattie, ran the store and they furnished some little farmers. Nathan Cartwright got all of his groceries and everything from Mr. Charlie and Miss Mattie there at the store.

When it came time to straighten out the account, it was just enough to pay out. He didn't have anything left. He said he couldn't figure out how he didn't get anything. He said Miss Mattie said, "Nathan, I'm going to tell you something and don't you ever forget it: furnish all, take all." He said after that he rented his land and got his money up front. He said he'd buy and sell horses, cows or do something, but Miss Mattie had broke him of farming.

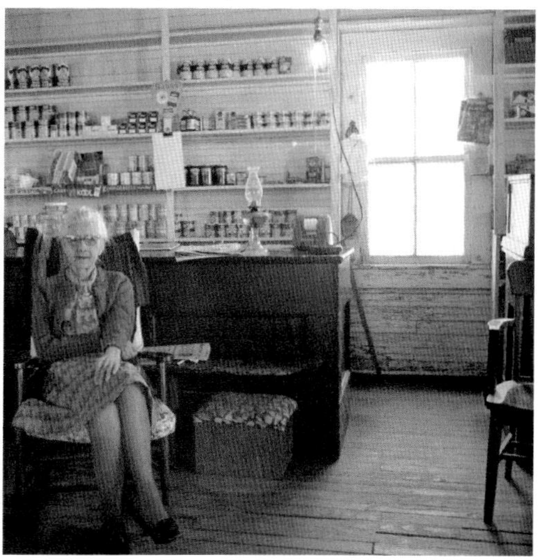

Miss Mattie Wright in her store in Jarvisburg. She was eighty-six when this picture was taken. She was Mr. Charlie Wright's wife and Dr. Charles and Caroline Wright's mother. *Courtesy of Caroline Wright.*

# Knotts Island

When I was a little boy, I used to go to Knotts Island every Memorial Day with Daddy and Mama. Daddy was always in politics, and every Memorial Day all the politicians went to the Methodist church on Knotts Island. They made speeches and had dinner on the grounds. Daddy always had to make a speech. I remember the road to the Pungo Ferry would sometimes be underwater if the tide was high. Back then, there was a cable ferry. It had a winch that would pull it from one side to the other. I think it had a six-cylinder Chevrolet engine turning the winch.

I know my daddy had a lot of good friends on Knotts Island, but I'm not going to begin to start calling names because I'd be sure to leave somebody out and I wouldn't want to do that.

When I decided to write a third book, I knew I wanted to include Knotts Island. My first thought was to call Joe Lewark. I got to know him when he was superintendent of Swan Island Club. I knew he was retired now, so I gave him a call and told him what I was doing. We set a date. I told him I needed to have a lot of pictures. He said he'd go through and get out what he thought I'd be interested in. When I got there, Joe introduced me to his wife, Carol, who I found to be a delightful person. She fixed a fresh pot of coffee and she had just made an apple cake. I'm a little diabetic and I'm not supposed to eat a lot of sweets, but I told her to bring that cake on. It was really good.

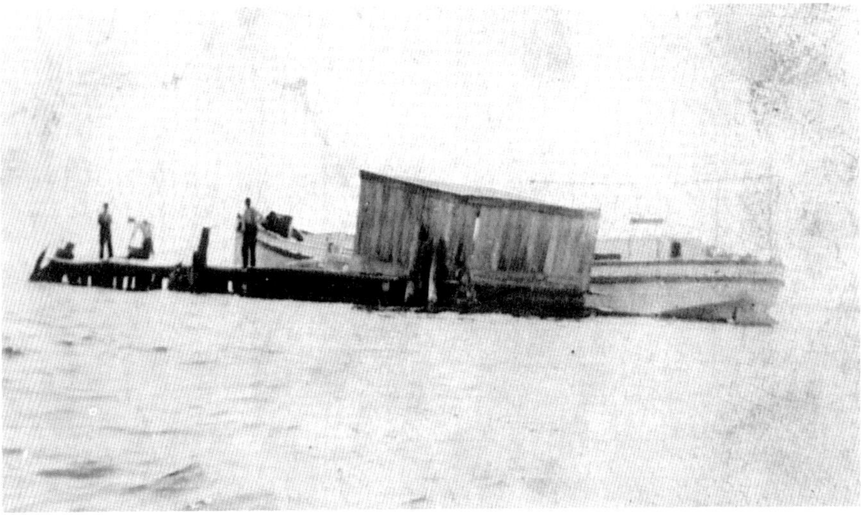

A freight boat loading at an old pier head at the south end of Knotts Island. *Courtesy of Joe Lewark.*

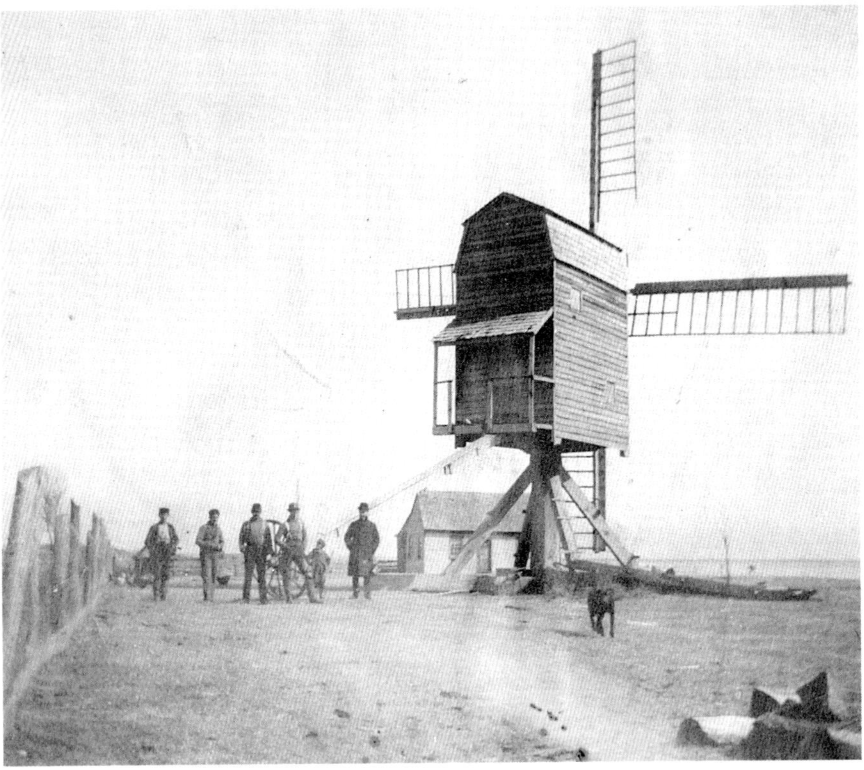

Pledge Ballance (nicknamed "Peel") at the gristmill where the ferry dock at Knotts Island is now. *Courtesy of Joe Lewark.*

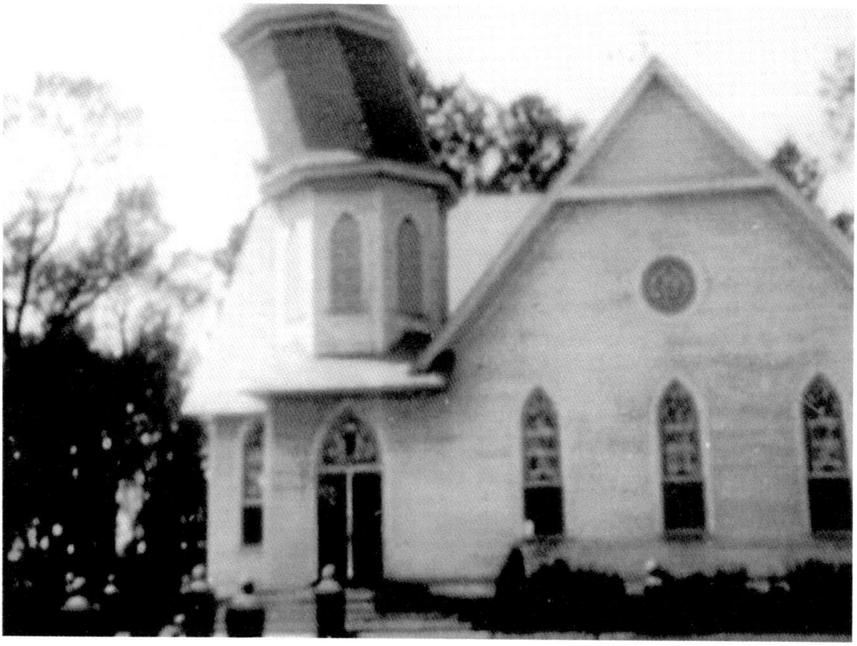

The Methodist church at Knotts Island after the 1933 hurricane. *Courtesy of Joe Lewark.*

Joe had lots of pictures, which he was kind enough to let me see and take to the office for copying. When I went to take Joe's pictures back, Bob Timberlake (the well-known artist) stopped by to see Joe and Carol. He is a member of Swan Island Club and he and a friend had been there hunting. Joe had sold him 167 old decoys. Thanks to Carol, he bought each of my books. He said it would give him something to read going home. There again, you never know who ducks will introduce you to.

Joe Lewark has made his living his whole life from the water of Currituck Sound. He has fished, crabbed, eeled, guided sportsmen on his own, was superintendent of Currituck Gunning and Fishing Club and was superintendent of Swan Island Club. For three years after high school, in the late 1950s, he guided sportsmen for Currituck Gunning and Fishing Club. The club was owned then by the Atlantic Gulf Stevedoran Company. After that, he ran his own rig for Miss Grace Williams on Knotts Island for nearly ten years. Then he and his brother Ralph started their own hunting and fishing lodge on the south end of the island and ran it from 1971 to 1988. During these years, Joe would commercial fish after the hunting season. He would go in with his fish at Knotts Island and drive all the way to Waterlily to sell them to Casey Jones (fifty to sixty miles, one way). He'd go back to Knotts Island and get up the next morning and do the same thing again.

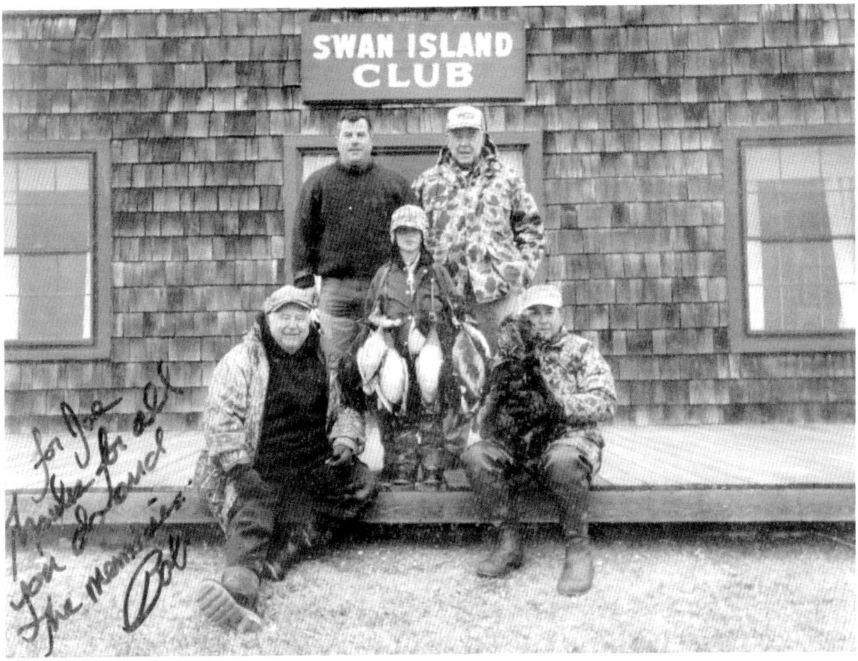


*Left to right:* Bob Timberlake, his son Dan, his grandson Deck, Joe Lewark and Ronnie Wade. *Courtesy of Joe Lewark.*

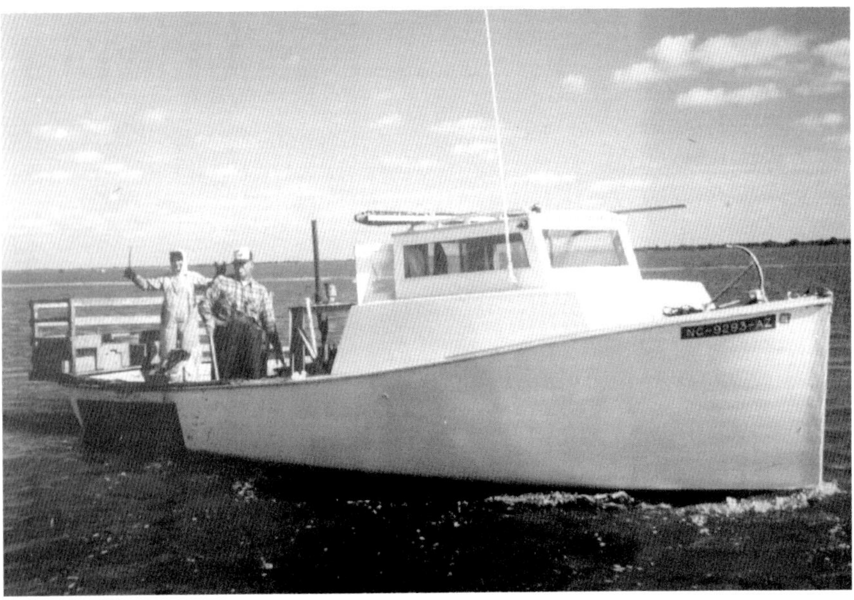

Joe and Carol Lewark crabbing. *Courtesy of Joe Lewark.*

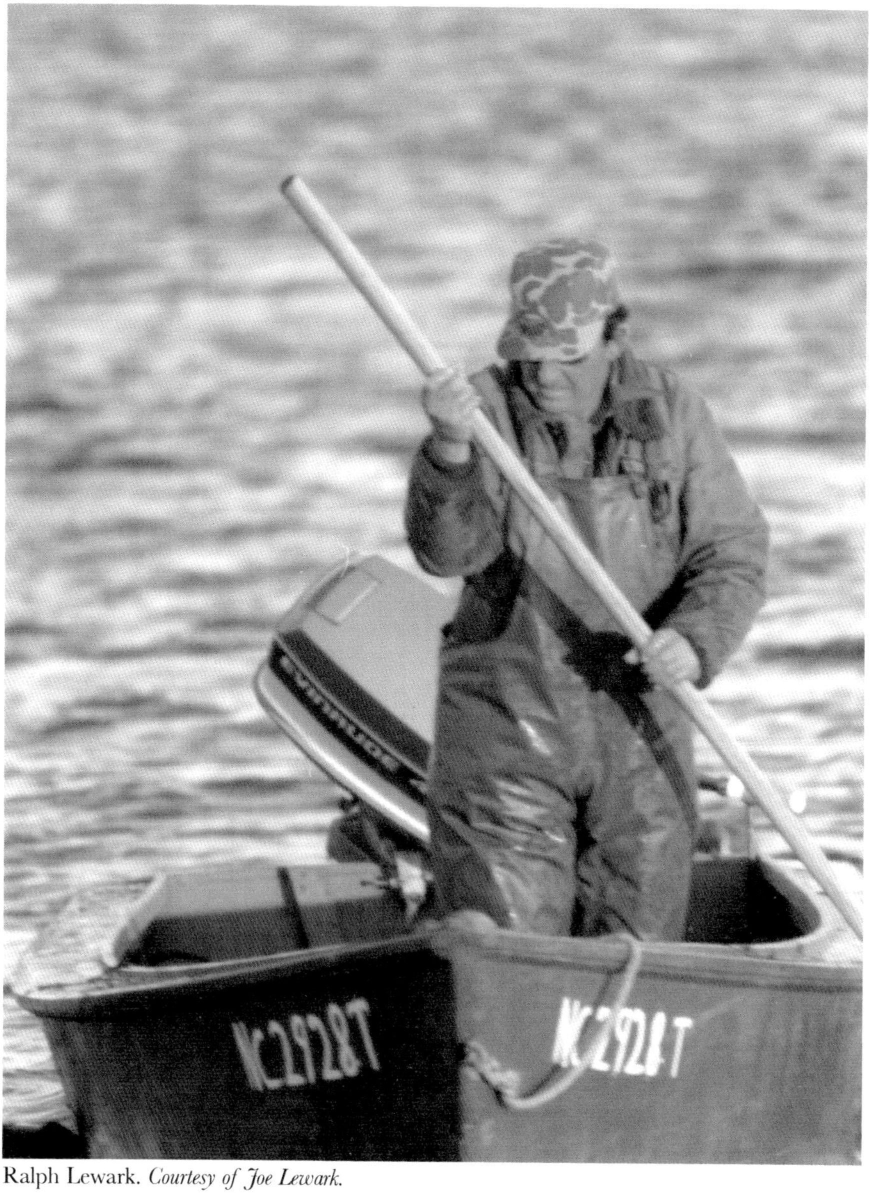


Ralph Lewark. *Courtesy of Joe Lewark.*

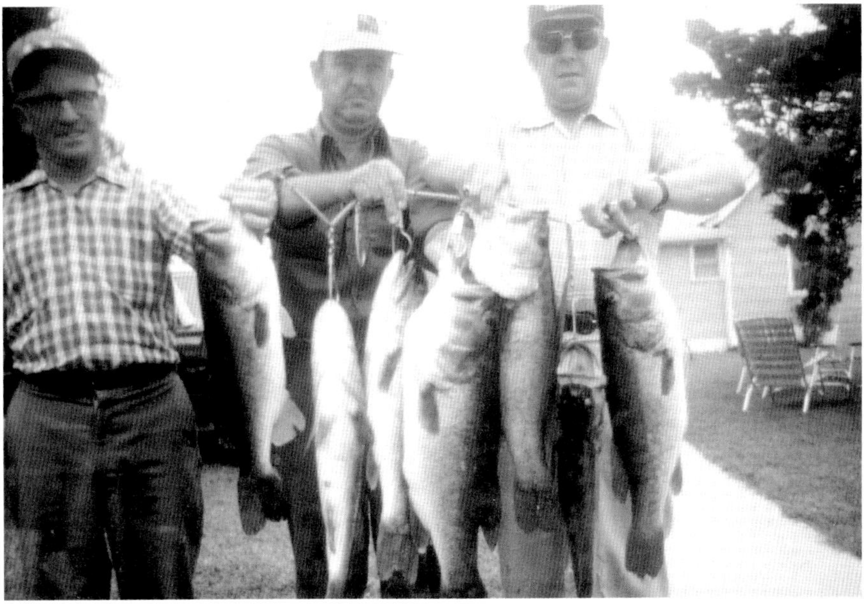

*Left to right:* Ed Fentress, Ralph Lewark and Joe Lewark in September of 1974. *Courtesy of Joe Lewark.*

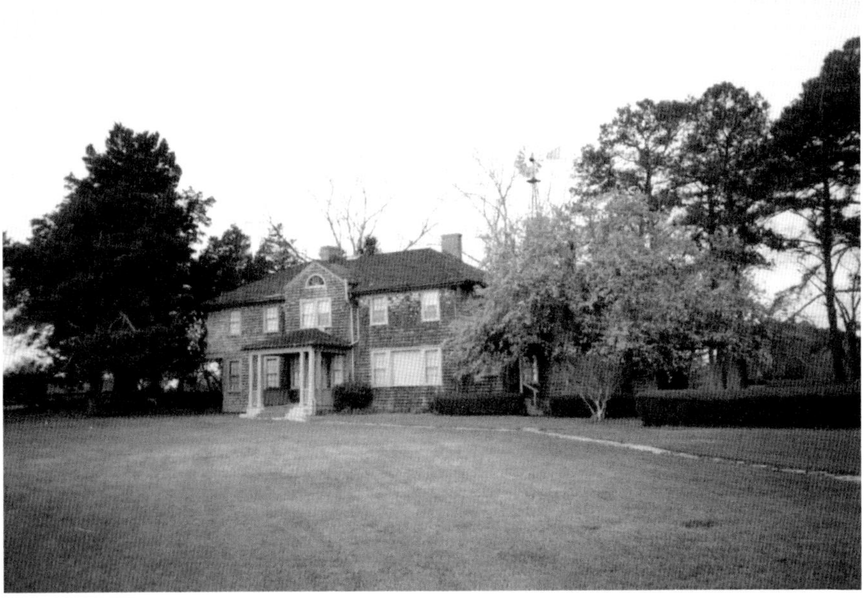

Currituck Gunning and Fishing Club on Knotts Island. *Courtesy of Joe Lewark.*

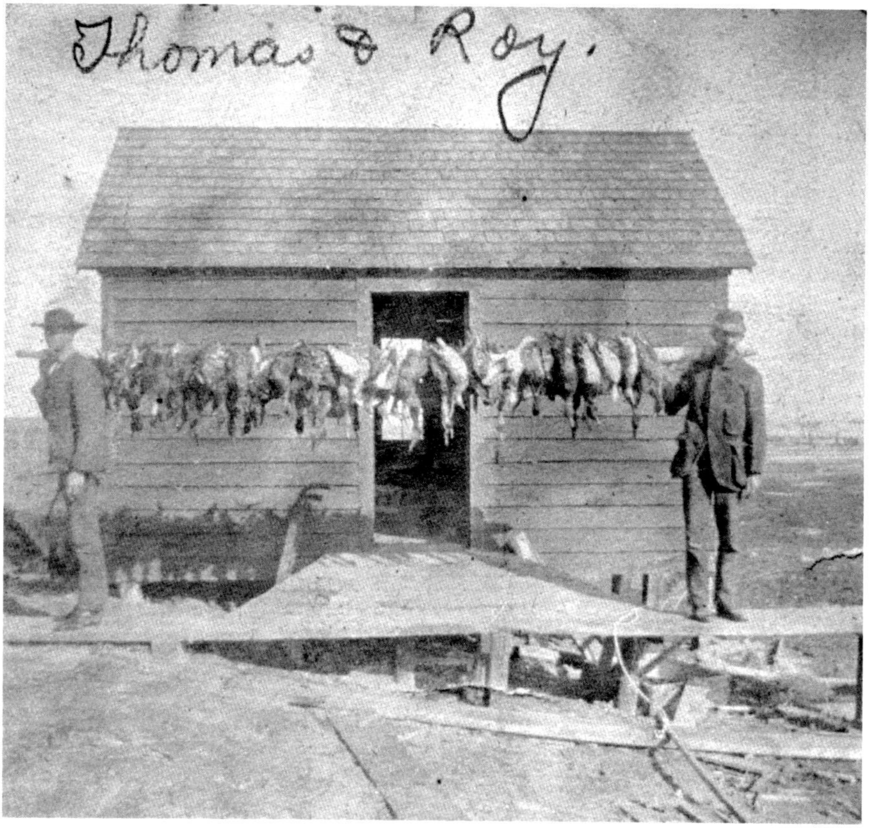


Thomas Waterfield (right). Currituck Gunning and Fishing Club in Knotts Island in 1910. *Courtesy of Joe Lewark.*

When Ralph's health got bad in 1998, Joe started managing Currituck Gunning and Fishing Club with his wife, Carol. At that time, it was owned by a group from Warrenton, Virginia. When the group put the club on the market, he went to Swan Island, where he was superintendent from 1994 to 2005, when he retired. Swan Island was originally owned by the Hatfields and was originally called "Crow Island."

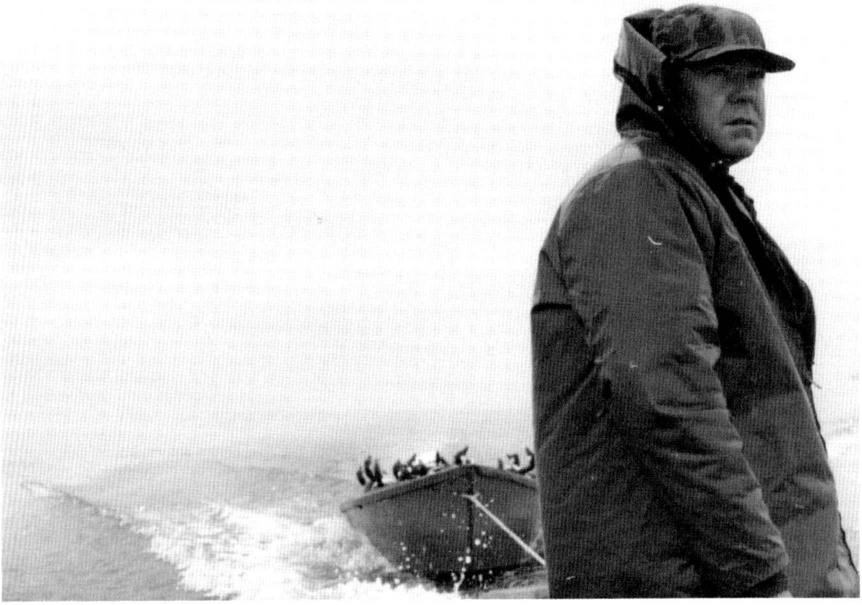

Joe Lewark pulling a skiffload of decoys in 1974. *Courtesy of Joe Lewark.*

# Decoys

Joe has owned as many valuable decoys as anybody I know. When he was at Swan Island, one of the members of the club, Vince Colson, gave him a bunch of field decoys that had been at the club since the early years. They were made by Lungren and were stuffed with wheat straw; they'd been bought at Abercrombie and Fitch in New York City.

There were some really old slat decoys (made with slats and covered with canvas). They were used with the battery rigs. Joe's were made by the famous carver Joe Lincoln. Joe Lewark had reheaded them. He had one with the original head. Joe got the decoys when the owners of Swan Island were going to burn them. A lot of them were sold to Bob Timberlake. One of them, a swan, sold to a collector in South Carolina for $16,000. Those decoys had horseshoes on the bottoms for weights. I remember that Mr. Pat O'Neal patterned his geese after those slat decoys and used them in his float-blind rig. When I was working for Mr. Pat, he sold his float rig to Swan Island Club and I painted those decoys before he delivered them.

Joe had a whole skiff rig of shorebirds that Mr. Timothy Bowden had given him when he got too old to hunt. He also had some Ned Burgess pintails and three shorebirds that Walter Jones had given him.

Back in the 1930s, Elmer Crowell had so many orders for decoys that he couldn't keep up, so he had to buy Mason heads.

The Forbes family was in the shipping business before it was in the publishing business. Some of them were original members of Swan Island

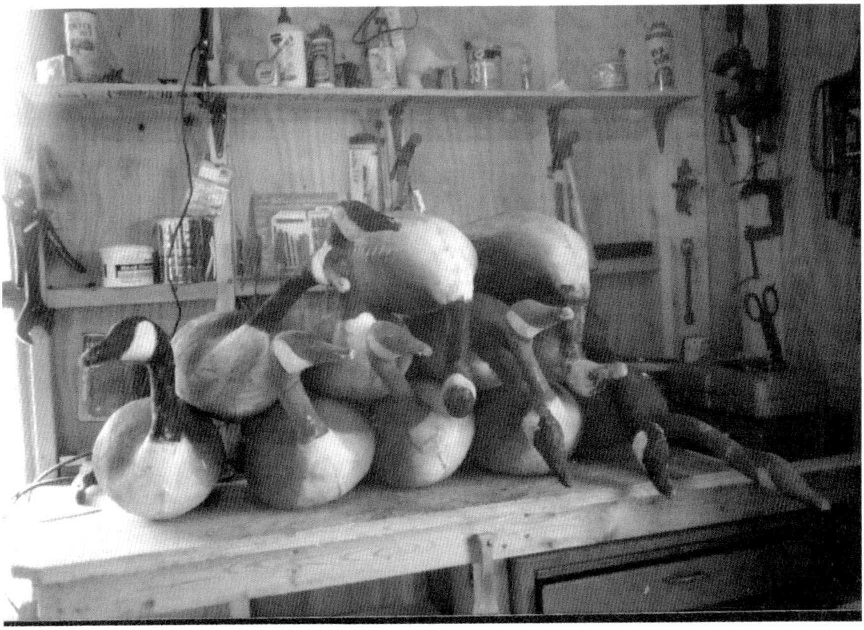

Goose decoys stuffed with wheat straw. *Courtesy of Joe Lewark.*

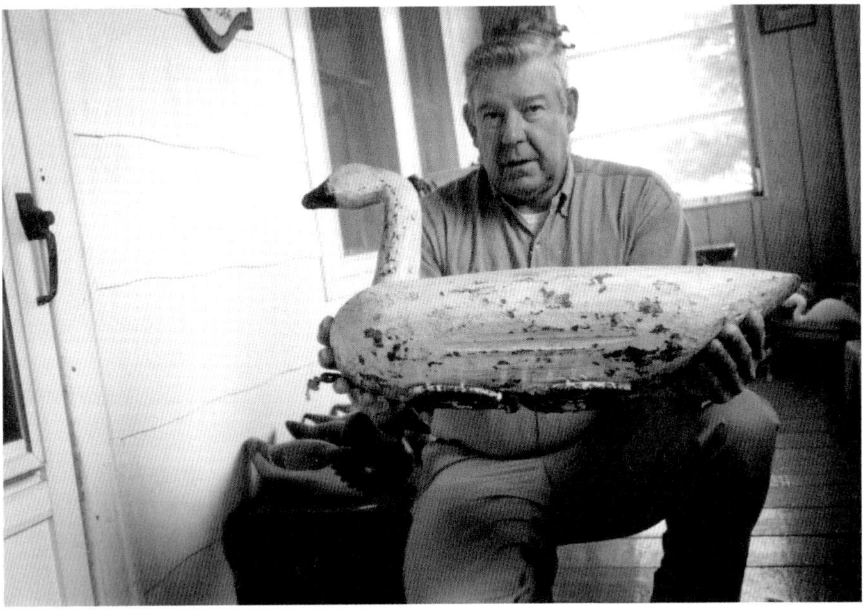

Joe Lewark holding the swan decoy that sold at the Timberlake sale for $16,000. *Courtesy of Joe Lewark.*

Club, after one of their ships came in through the old Currituck Inlet to get out of a bad storm in the early 1870s.

Joe talked about a bunch of old ducks attributed to that original Forbes ship from Long Island, New York. Two wedge tails have "W.H. Forbes" on the bottom of them. They never could trace them back to the carvers but figured maybe the carpenters on the ship made them in the off-season. William Hathaway Forbes was in the original Swan Island Club. He was in the Civil War as an officer and wound up in one of the stockades in Georgia that was so bad. In a swap, he got out of there. He went back to serve and was at Appomattox with Grant and Lee.

# Swan Island

In 1976, I was asked by the Currituck County Historical Society to write the histories of Swan Island, Monkey Island, Whalehead and Narrows Island Clubs. Since Swan Island was very closely associated with the people on Knotts Island, I think it is appropriate for me to include its history in this book. I do so with the permission of the Currituck County Historical Society.

In 1872, a group of men left Long Island on a schooner to go to Florida to duck hunt. When they got off the North Carolina coast, they ran into a September storm and came into Old Inlet and anchored to the leeward of Swan Island.

When the storm was over, the schooner was aground. A man named Hatfield, who owned Swan Island at the time, talked them into staying there and hunting in the winter of 1872. They lived on the schooner. They stayed on her for seven years during hunting seasons. After the season was over, of course, they would go back to New York. The bottom of the boat is there now, just to the east of the clubhouse.

Mr. Hatfield took care of the schooner for them when they were in New York, until 1879, when she burned. Then the group bought Swan Island itself, which contained about 126 acres. They kept buying marsh until they had approximately 10,000 acres. Mr. J.M. Wade, the present superintendent (then 1976) of the club, doesn't know just how it came about, but a group of men from Boston later got control of Swan Island Club.

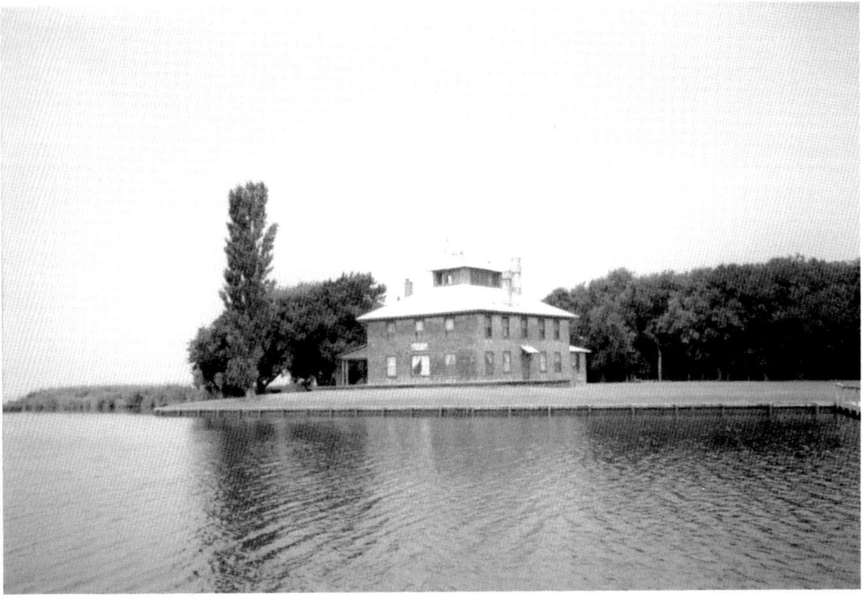

Swan Island Club. *Courtesy of Joe Lewark.*

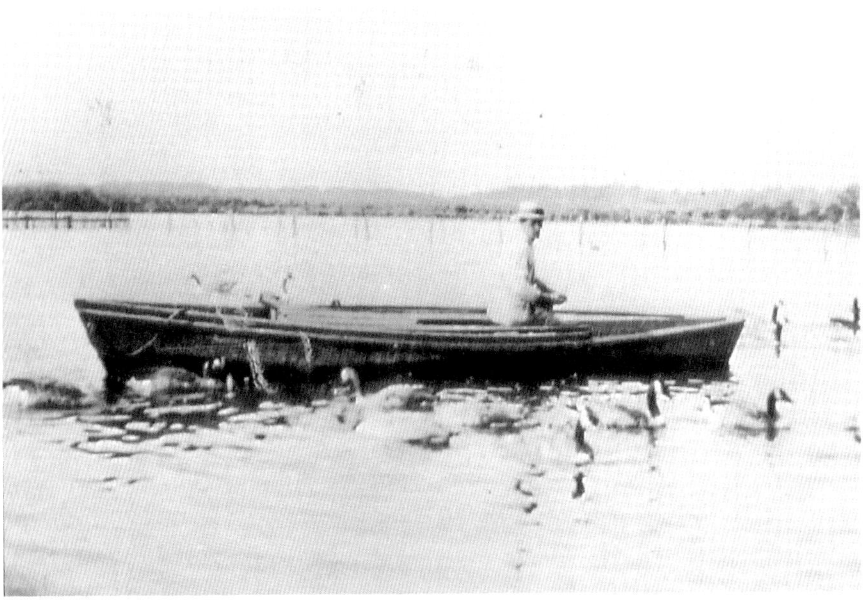

Pud White feeding live goose decoys. *Courtesy of Joe Lewark.*

Today, there are still many pictures of the old members hanging on the wall in the club. There used to be a rule that when a member died or got out of the club, his picture was hung the next year. You couldn't sell your right in the club. If you died or wanted to get out, your interest reverted back to the club. Then if the members chose to take in another person, they could do so. In later years, that rule changed and that is when the club started going down, according to Mr. Wade. In 1920, some New Yorkers got back in the club. Then, as they died and their heirs had no interest in hunting, they forced the sale of it in about 1968. At that time, all the Northern people sold out to a group of local people around Virginia Beach and Richmond. These people didn't hunt at all for about three years. They were more interested in the development of the beach property. What are now Swan Beach and North Swan Beach Developments were originally mostly Swan Island Club property. After about 1971, the owners got interested in hunting and have opened it to the public on a limited basis. This was not the first time it was open to the public. It had been open on a limited basis by some of the previous owners.

Mr. Wade's father went to work at Swan Island in 1916 as a marsh guard and continued to work there until 1955. Mr. J.M. Wade retired from the Coast Guard and went to work at Swan Island as a guide in 1955. He was made superintendent in 1957. Some of the earlier superintendents were: Mr. Williams, followed by Mr. George Cason, then his son Lindy Cason and then Mr. Wendell Waterfield, who was superintendent just before Mr. J.M. Wade.

The present clubhouse is the third one that has been on Swan Island. Mr. Wade doesn't know how old it is, but said he was sixty-five (in 1976) and can just remember when it was built. He said one Sunday morning after it was finished, all the people on Knotts Island who had worked on the house brought their families over to look at it. Mr. Wade said it was really something to speak about in those days.

The clubhouse has seven bedrooms, three bedrooms for cooks, a large clubroom with a fireplace, a kitchen and a dining room. It has two main floors with a large cupola above the second floor. The men could go up there and look out all over the marsh and decide where they wanted to go hunting. There is a secret wall panel in the club room that opens. This is where the club members kept their liquor during Prohibition days. They have a mounted albino widgeon and also an albino teal. They say there have only been two albino teal known to have been killed in the United States—this one and one in California. There is a board over the fireplace with the inscription:

> *ILLE TERRARVM MIHI PRAETER OMNES ANGVLVS RIDET*

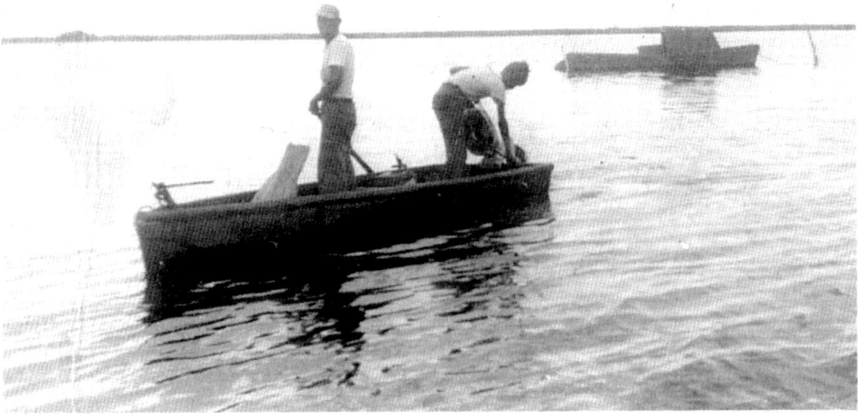

Lundy Cason and son Jimmy in the late 1940s in a skiff that Will White built out of pine. She had a ten-horsepower Mercury motor on her. *Courtesy of Joe Lewark.*

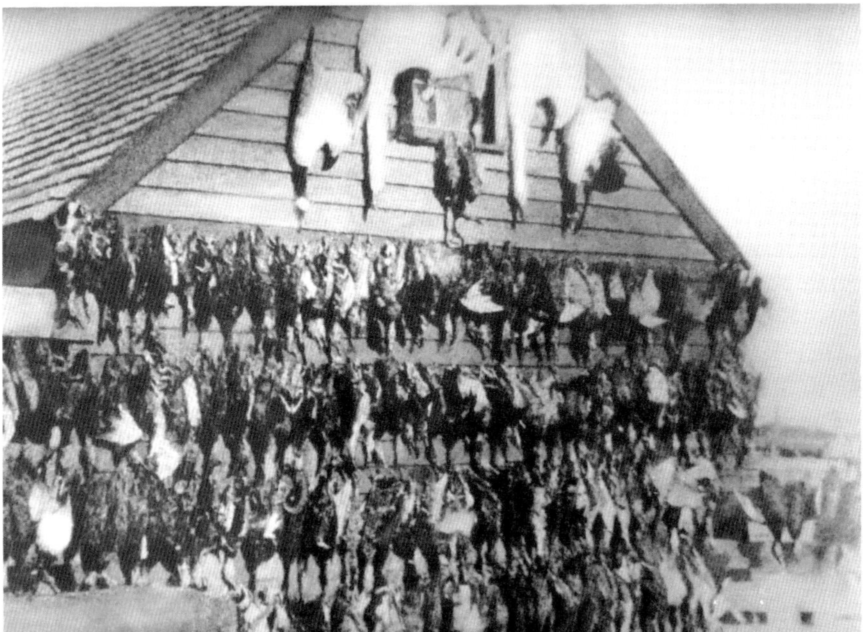

Big kill at Swan Island on November 11, 1901, in North Raymonds Pond. Hunters stopped shooting at 2:30 p.m. with 165 ducks and 1 goose. Total killed that day out of 5 blinds was 414 ducks. *Courtesy of Joe Lewark.*

Mr. Wade says there have been many interpretations of this and it is thought to be Latin, but basically what it means is, "This place appeals to me more than any place on earth." Mr. Wade's father told him that one of the old members was going out to the bay one morning and picked up this board. He started carving on it, and when he left he put the board in his sea chest until he came back the next year. He did this for about four years until he completed it.

The bedrooms each have an old, iron wood stove, and originally each member had a guide assigned to him. The guide would go in early mornings and build the fire. When the room got warm, the sportsman would get up and dress. There is also a house for guide's quarters, a generator house and a boathouse on the island.

Mr. Wade said he used to have an old man and his wife who came down and brought another couple with them and stayed for ten days. When he came, he said, "Mike, I don't want to be bothered unless some member of my immediate family dies, and don't bring me any newspapers. Some mornings when you come over I may not speak to you, but don't feel hard. Keep the guides around just in case I want to ask them something." Sometimes he would stay the whole ten days and pay the price of ten guests, but never go hunting.

Then Mr. Wade said he used to have an old man that "came a hollering drunk and left a hollering drunk," but the man said when he came: "Mike, I came down here to get away and have a good time. If I tear up anything or break anything, or cause any trouble, let me know and I'll pay for it when I leave."

Mr. Wade says the farther north you go the better the men are to work for. They may ask you to do things out of the ordinary, and they will let you know they are Northerners, but when they leave, they will pay you for it.

One time, Mr. Wade had a guide helping him and the sportsman kept calling the guide "boy." He would say, "Boy, do this" or "Boy, do that." The guide went to Mr. Wade and said he just couldn't take that man calling him "boy." Mr. Wade said, "As long as he takes care of me when he leaves he can call me anything he wants to."

Mr. Wade said if he had all the old decoys that used to be there, it's hard to tell what they'd be worth today. There is a beautiful swan decoy in the clubhouse now, and Mr. Wade remembers his father talking about chopping up swan decoys like this for firewood after it became illegal to hunt swan.

Swan Island is still a beautiful place and the clubhouse is kept in a good state of repair. I hope the owners will continue to maintain it because places like this are fast disappearing in Currituck. I am indebted to Mr. J.M. Wade of Knotts Island for all the information I have written about Swan Island Club (in 1976).

I'm pleased to say that, as of this writing in 2007, Swan Island Club is still kept up and run as the old clubs were run.

# Ducks Demand a Road

Before Chory's Hunting Lodge opened on Knotts Island, there was no road across the marsh and everyone had to get there by boat. Part of the deal when Mr. Chory opened his hunting lodge was that he would dredge canals through the marsh and put in a punching road (logs laid crossways) across the marsh. These roads required a lot of maintenance, so every man had to work for one day a month to maintain it. If he didn't, he was fined. If you had a horse, the horse counted as a worker. With the road in place, Mr. Knapp and all the owners of hunting and fishing lodges could get their folks in to hunt and fish without having to pick them up by boat at Munden's Point.

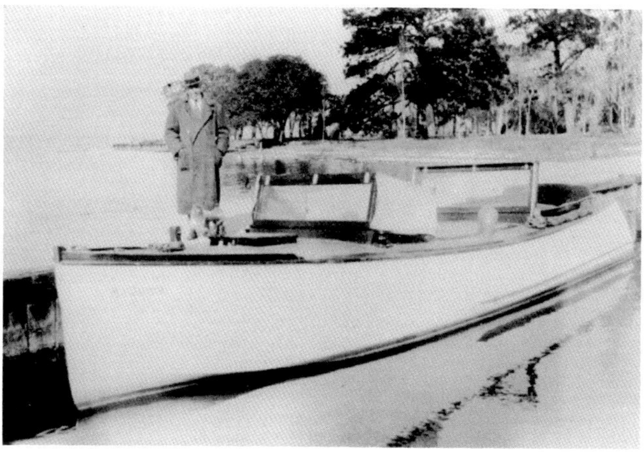

Mr. Joseph Palmer Knapp, who owned Mackey Island, and his boat *Le Mer* that he had brought down from New York. *Courtesy of Joe Lewark.*

# Mutiny in Virginia

Joe told me about the hunters in Virginia using little decoys, while the folks in Currituck used big decoys. Back in the market-hunting days, hunters from Currituck would slip up into Sandbridge and Princess Anne Club territory and put the Virginia hunters to shame. He said it was like the oyster wars in Tangier. Like mutiny.

I asked Joe more about the carvers on Knotts Island and he said there were a lot of people who made them, but they were mostly making them for their own use. George Waterfield made a lot of decoys for battery rigs. He said most of the decoys the Dudleys made were for people up in Back Bay. After that, the carvers were making mostly show birds. Curtis, Wayne, Ronnie and Fred Waterfield made them. Joe said his daddy, Fred Lewark, produced some of the first canvas geese that were made after live decoys were outlawed. He made several stands for people around there. Those producing decoys back then were making them as a working tool. They would never have guessed that their working tools would turn into collectibles bringing more income per decoy than they earned in a year of hard work.

# John Barnes

I've known John Barnes for at least twenty-five years. He was on the Currituck Board of Education when my first wife, Frances, was on the board and he's still serving on it.

When John High and I started Piney Island Club in 1983, Jack Laughery (CEO of Imasco Ltd., U.S.A., Hardee's parent company) was an original member. The point here is that Hardee's used to take a party to the Barnes Lodge on Knotts Island. I remember them talking about all the food Mrs. Barnes (John's mother) served them. My good friend DeWitt McCotter, who was their attorney, was with them on several of those hunting trips. Now, McCotter is not fat. I don't know where the food goes, but that man can put some food away. On one of those trips to the Barnes Lodge, they weighed him before supper and after supper. He gained six pounds. John said they've been cooking the same menu for fifty years or more. It must work! John said they can't guarantee ducks, but they can guarantee food.

Mr. Mike Wade, who was superintendent of Swan Island Club in 1976, told me that as long as you give a man a good, dry place to sleep, good food, good liquor and a good oak fire, you are not going to have much trouble with him. I've found that to be true.

John told me his daddy was a federal game warden in the late 1920s and early 1930s. They started the lodge in the 1930s. Another old lodge at Knotts Island was the Williamses'. It was started not long after the Barnses'.

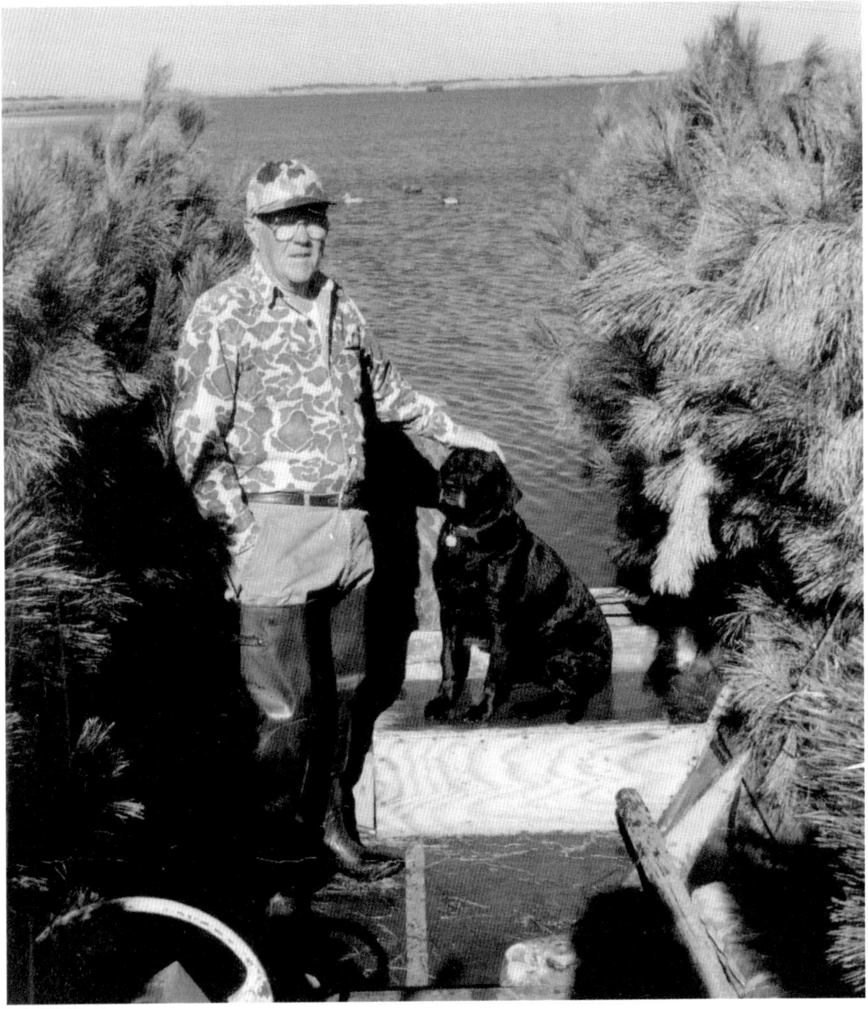

John Barnes and his dog in a duck blind. *Courtesy of John Barnes.*

I asked John about some of the people who had guided for him. He said going way back there was Elmer Sawyer, Ralph Lewark, Jimmy Cason, Billy Cason, Calvin Sawyer (he was from Manns Harbor and guided for them for about twenty years), Cale Hardison and others he couldn't think of. He said all his blinds are open-water blinds.

There used to be a bombing target in Currituck Sound. John said this plane was doing night runs on the target and the pilots flew the plane right into the water. This was February 5, 1950. He said it was cold and making ice when they got a call from the duty officer at Oceana wanting to know if they had heard any unusual noises. They hadn't, but walked out on the

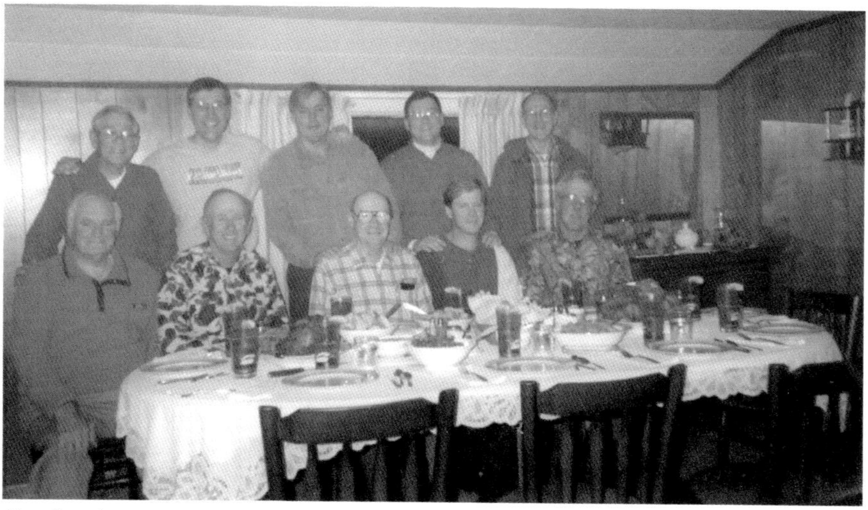

Gore hunting party getting ready for one of Mrs. Barnes's famous meals. *Courtesy of John Barnes.*

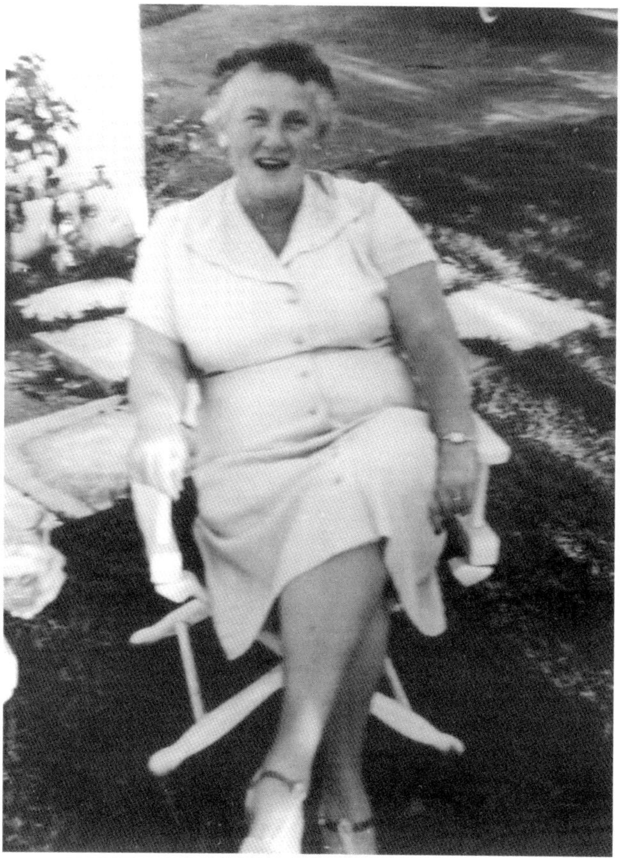

Frances Barnes.
*Courtesy of John Barnes.*

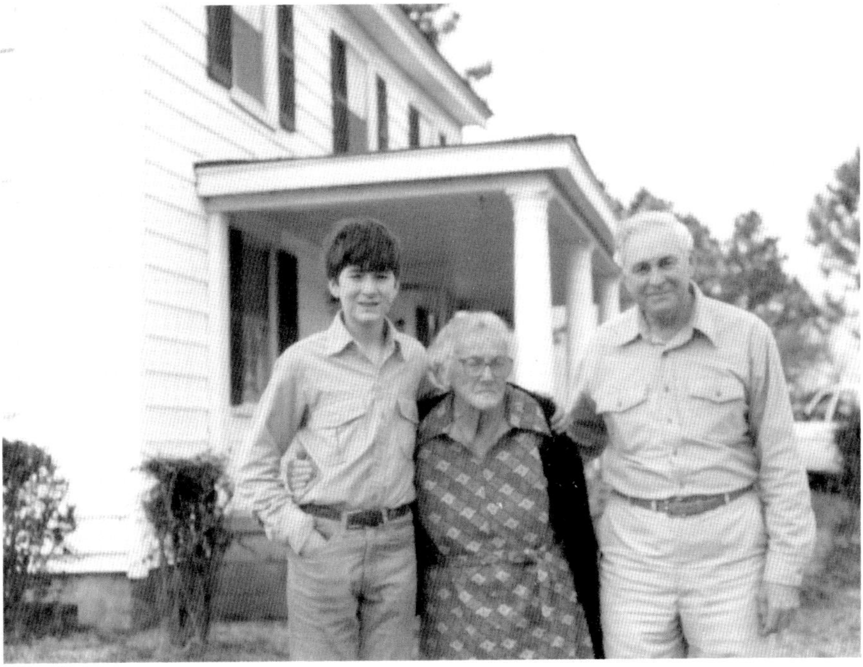

*Left to right:* Grover Gore Jr., Mrs. Barnes and Grover Gore Sr. Grover Sr. is an attorney from Southport, North Carolina. He has been bringing a party to the Barnes Lodge every year, longer than any of their other parties. *Courtesy of John Barnes.*

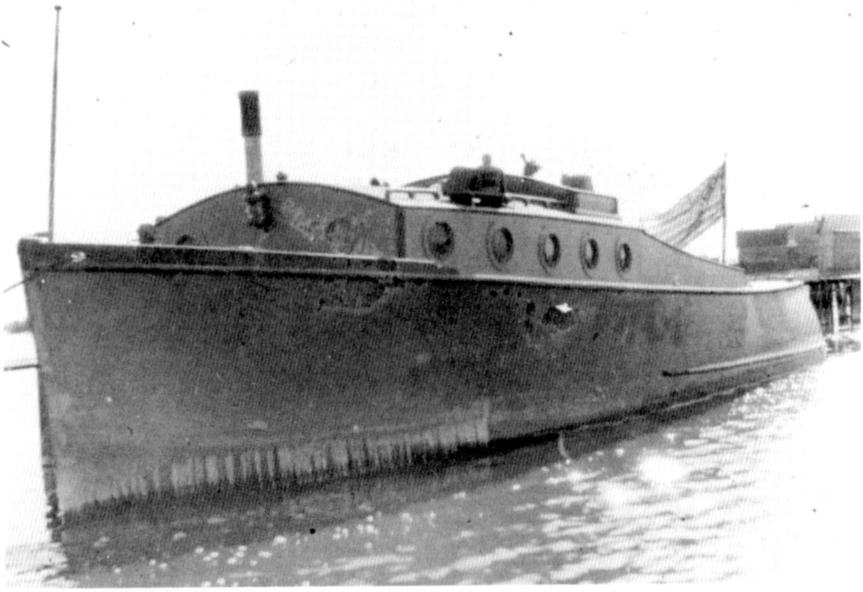

Federal game warden boat. Note the icicles hanging from the bow and the flag flying at stern. *Courtesy of John Barnes.*

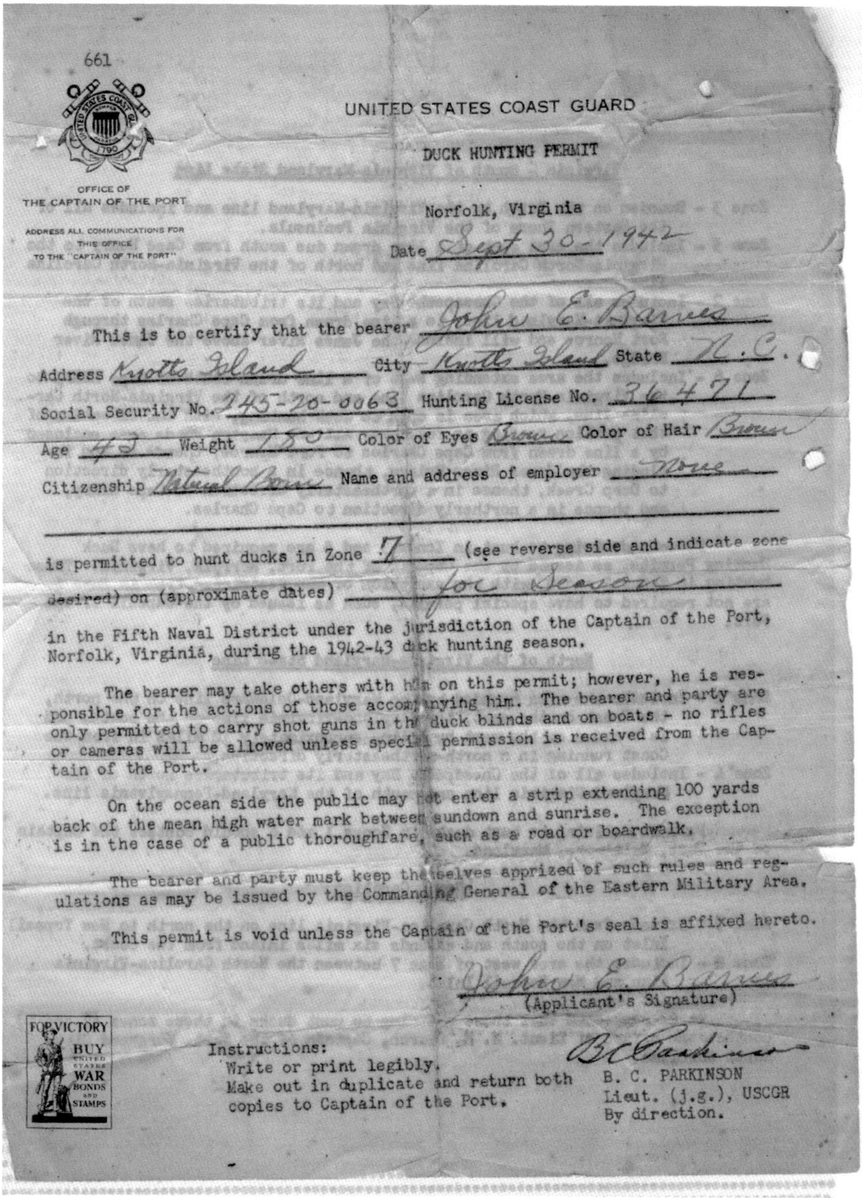

661

UNITED STATES COAST GUARD

OFFICE OF THE CAPTAIN OF THE PORT

ADDRESS ALL COMMUNICATIONS FOR THIS OFFICE TO THE "CAPTAIN OF THE PORT"

DUCK HUNTING PERMIT

Norfolk, Virginia

Date Sept 30-1942

This is to certify that the bearer John E. Barnes

Address Knotts Island City Knotts Island State N.C.

Social Security No. 245-20-0063 Hunting License No. 36471

Age 43 Weight 180 Color of Eyes Brown Color of Hair Brown

Citizenship Natural Born Name and address of employer None

is permitted to hunt ducks in Zone 7 (see reverse side and indicate zone desired) on (approximate dates) for Season

in the Fifth Naval District under the jurisdiction of the Captain of the Port, Norfolk, Virginia, during the 1942-43 duck hunting season.

The bearer may take others with him on this permit; however, he is responsible for the actions of those accompanying him. The bearer and party are only permitted to carry shot guns in the duck blinds and on boats - no rifles or cameras will be allowed unless special permission is received from the Captain of the Port.

On the ocean side the public may not enter a strip extending 100 yards back of the mean high water mark between sundown and sunrise. The exception is in the case of a public thoroughfare, such as a road or boardwalk.

The bearer and party must keep themselves apprized of such rules and regulations as may be issued by the Commanding General of the Eastern Military Area.

This permit is void unless the Captain of the Port's seal is affixed hereto.

John E. Barnes
(Applicant's Signature)

FOR VICTORY BUY UNITED STATES WAR BONDS AND STAMPS

Instructions:
Write or print legibly.
Make out in duplicate and return both copies to Captain of the Port.

B C Parkinson
B. C. PARKINSON
Lieut. (j.g.), USCGR
By direction.

During World War II, you had to have a permit from the Coast Guard to hunt ducks in Currituck Sound. This is John Sr.'s permit. *Courtesy of John Barnes.*

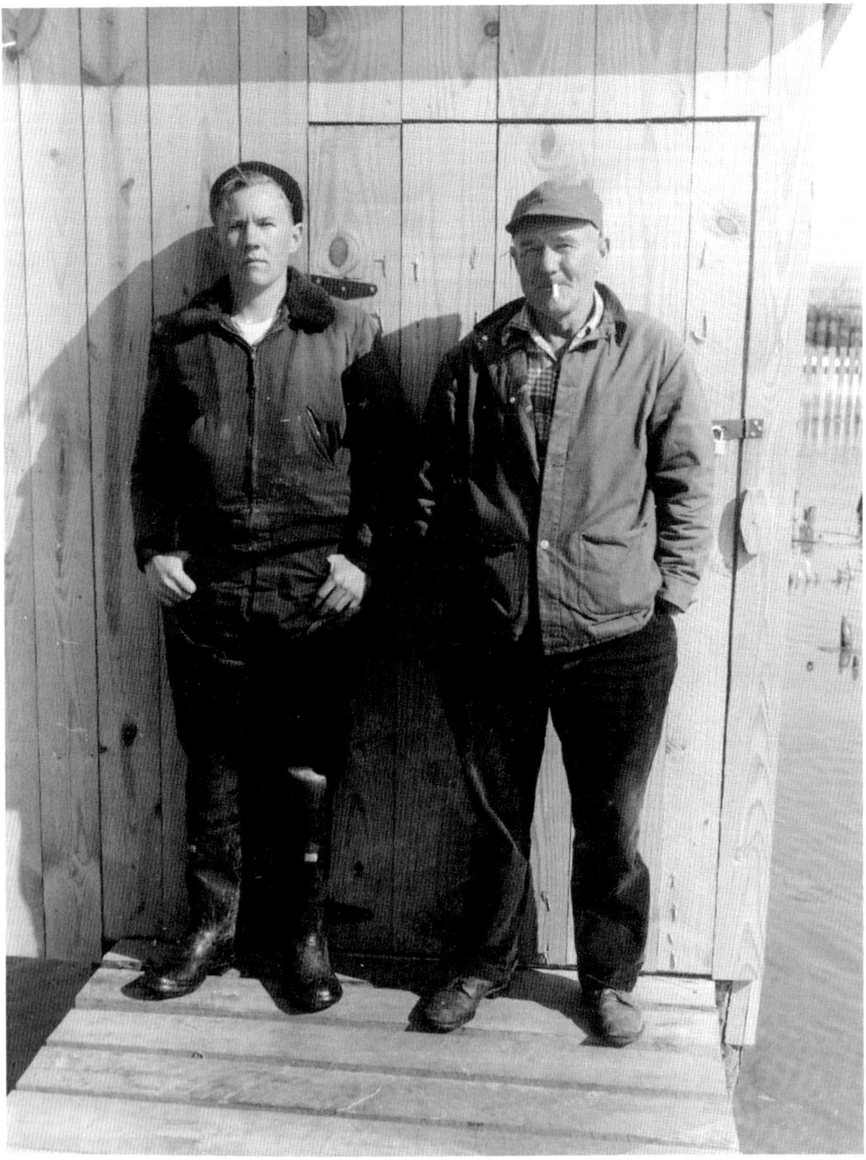

John Barnes and John Barnes Sr. This picture was taken by the navy after they rescued the pilots from a navy plane that went down in the freezing waters of Currituck Sound. *Courtesy of John Barnes.*

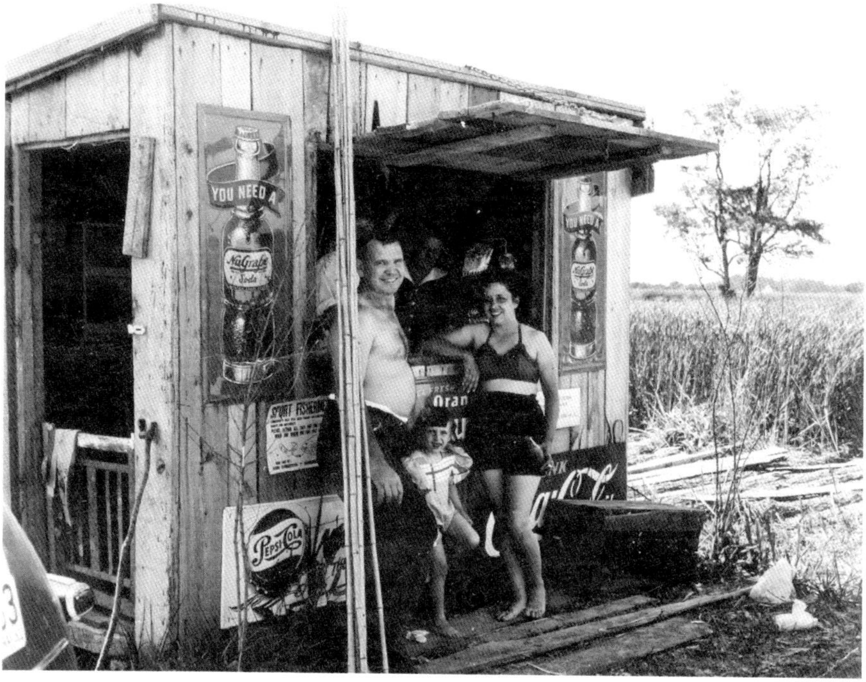


The Barnes Store at the south end of Knotts Island in 1956. *Courtesy of John Barnes.*

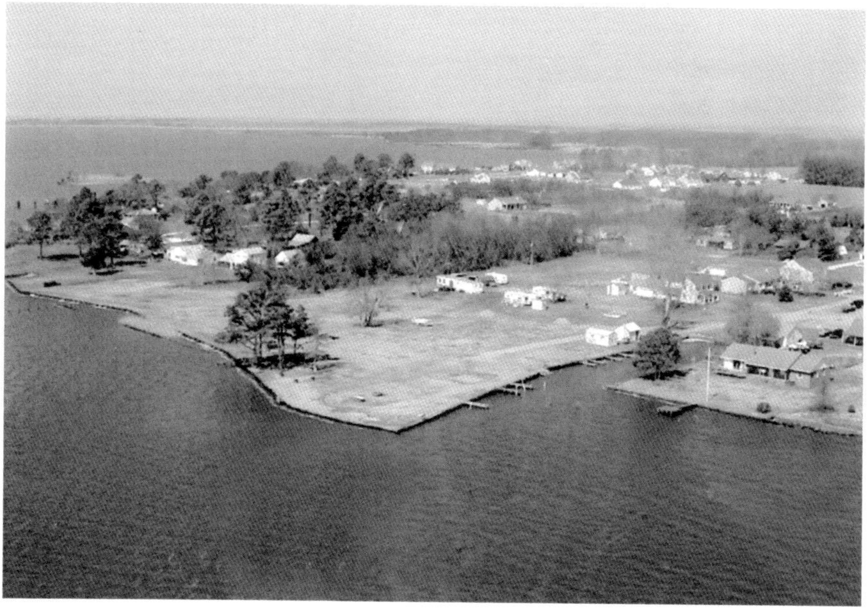

The Barnes Lodge on the south end of Knotts Island. *Courtesy of John Barnes.*

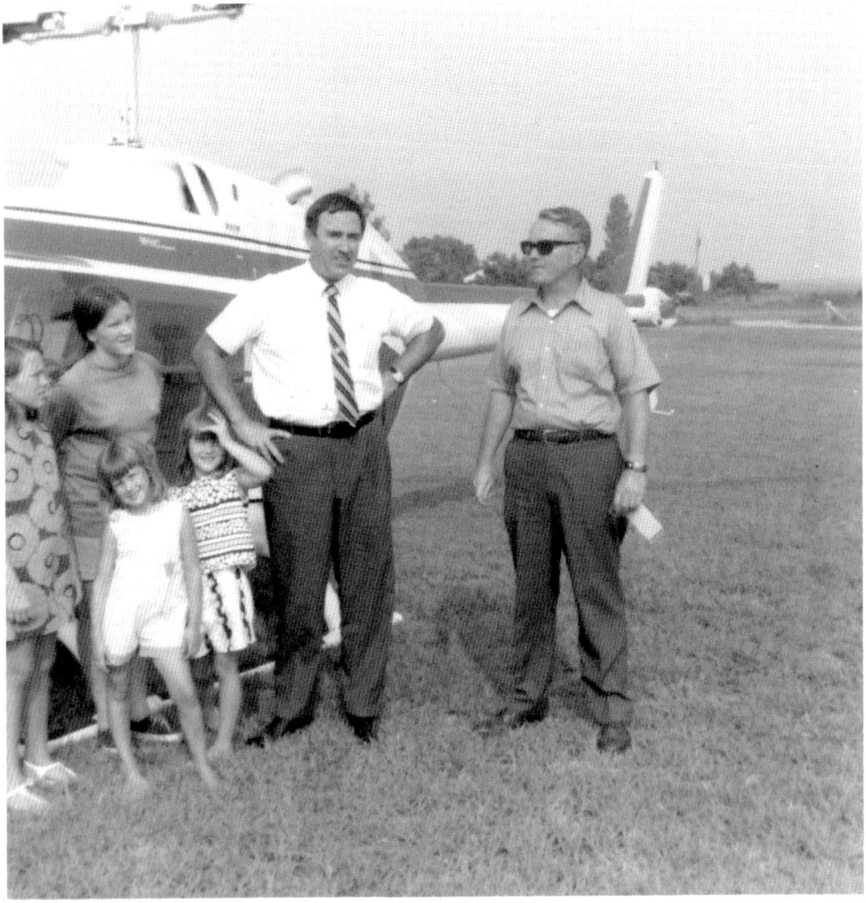

*Left to right:* Janet Williams, Donna Barnes McCloud, Molly Bright Williams, Tracy Bray Mason, Governor Bob Scott and John Barnes. *Courtesy of John Barnes.*

dock and just happened to see a flare. John said he and his daddy broke ice and went out there and got them. He said one had a bone sticking out of his leg, one had a broken back and there was a third. He said they were all just about frozen, but they all lived.

# Poplar Branch Landing

I remember Poplar Branch Landing in the late 1940s and early 1950s. This was a lively place. Mr. Norman Gregory bought fish there and sold all kinds of supplies to fishermen and hunters, such as net webbing, corks, lead, line, boat pumps, propellers and automotive parts. All the gas boats had car engines except some of the club boats that had marine engines. He also sold foul-weather gear. If he didn't have something you wanted, he'd have it by the next day. He sent a truck to Norfolk every day. He also sold gas. Laverne Brickhouse told me that if the sportsmen wanted the ducks they had killed sent to their homes up north, Mr. Norman would pack them in ice and send them on the truck to Norfolk, where they were sent on to their destination. She also told me that he had a gristmill. He would grind up corn for people and make meal. She said he sold fishing supplies to people all down the beach and as for south as Low Land, North Carolina. She said people from Virginia also came down here to buy supplies.

Mr. Norman furnished all the hunt clubs. He had a barge that he used for hauling wood for the fireplaces at Monkey Island, Whalehead, Currituck and Pine Island Clubs. He also delivered coal in burlap bags to the clubs that had coal furnaces. I know that Monkey Island and Whalehead did. They later converted the furnaces to oil and he delivered that as well. He also sold coal to homes in Currituck and all the way to Duck. He hauled corn to all the clubs on the barge to feed the ducks.

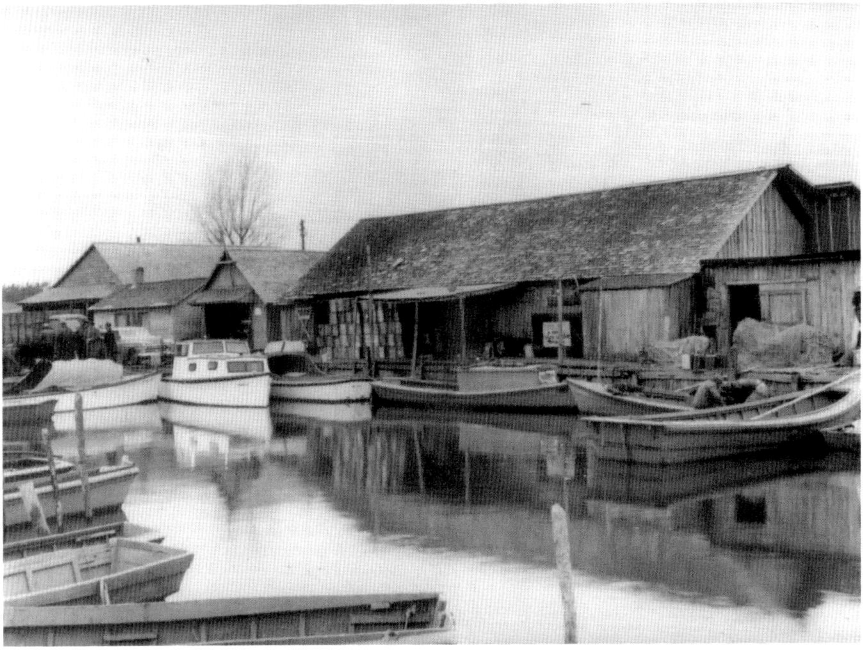

Poplar Branch Landing. The white boat on the far left belonged to Pine Island Club. Next was Whalehead Club's and then Currituck Club's. These boats were at Poplar Branch Landing to pick up sportsmen. The man working on the engine is Otto Bateman; the man standing, back to the camera, is Howard Sumrell. *Courtesy of Levie Bunch Jr.*

Mr. Jerry Bunch had a grocery store at Poplar Branch Landing and the clubs, except Monkey Island, bought their groceries and house supplies from him. This was big business. This was also the gathering place for folks to hang around and talk and get the news.

Pine Island, Whalehead and Currituck Clubs all picked up their sportsmen at Poplar Branch Landing. Monkey Island had its own dock at Waterlily. Also, they bought their groceries at Worth Guard's store in Coinjock during this period. Mr. Carl White was superintendent of Pine Island Club for thirty-eight years. He had Mr. Pat O'Neal build the club's boat. She was the first of many boats Mr. Pat built that had a concave tunnel. They ran good in shallow water and didn't cavitate like a box tunnel.

Mr. Dexter Snow was superintendent of Whalehead Club for all the years Mr. Ray Adams owned it except for the first winter. The first winter, Captain Neal and Miss Daisy Midgett (who owned the First Colony Inn Hotel in Nags Head) ran the club. My Daddy, Chester R. Morris, who was Mr. Adams's attorney, arranged that. Mr. Adams needed a boat, but he wouldn't pay the price Mr. Pat charged. His price was $100 per foot, plus all the hardware and engine. If you wanted a cabin, that was extra. Mr. Adams

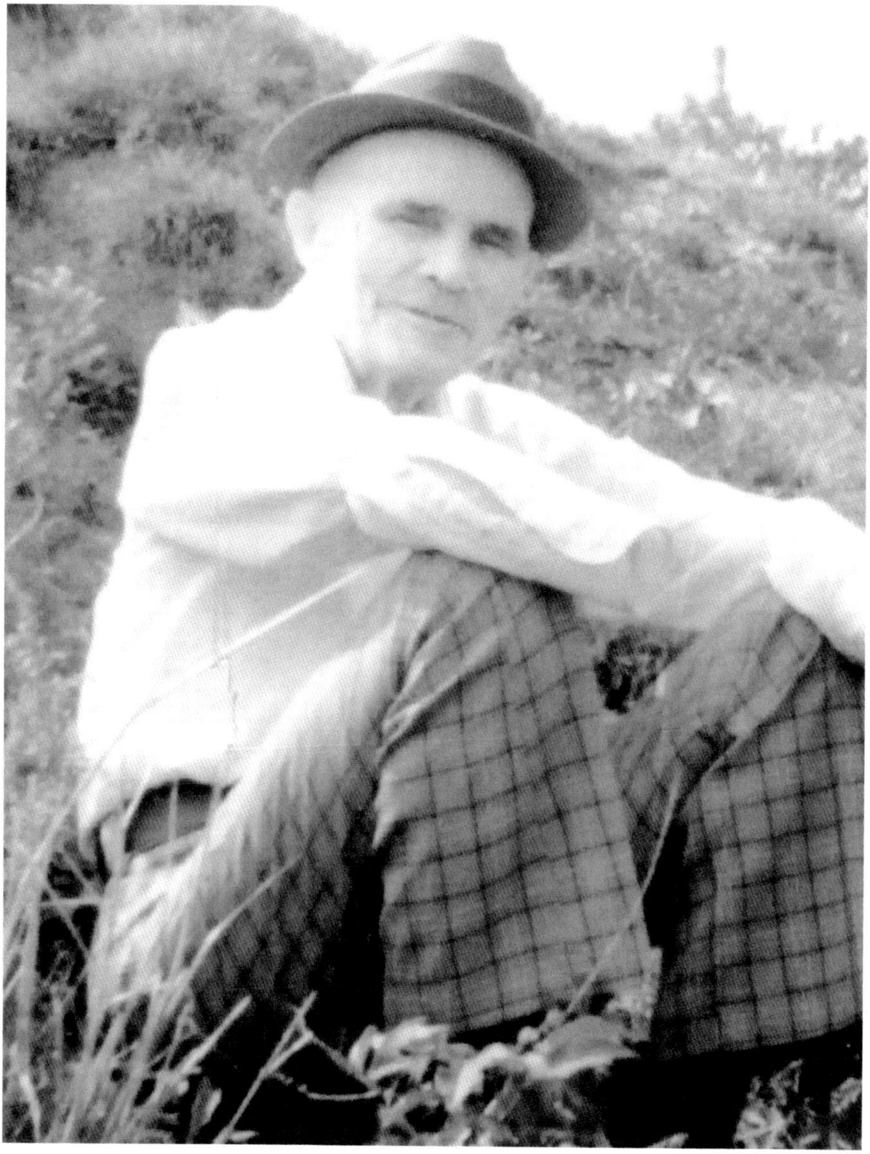

Jerry Bunch. *Courtesy of Olive Butt.*

had bought the abandoned Penny's Hill Coast Guard Station and moved it to the yard of the Whalehead Club. He got Mr. Albert Sumrell to build the boat in the boathouse part of the old station. Ambrose "Hambone" Twiford and I ended up with this boat in the early 1970s. We knocked the cabin and skeg off of her and used her as a barge to haul lumber to build the first two houses on the oceanfront in Corolla. Jimmy Hayman brought

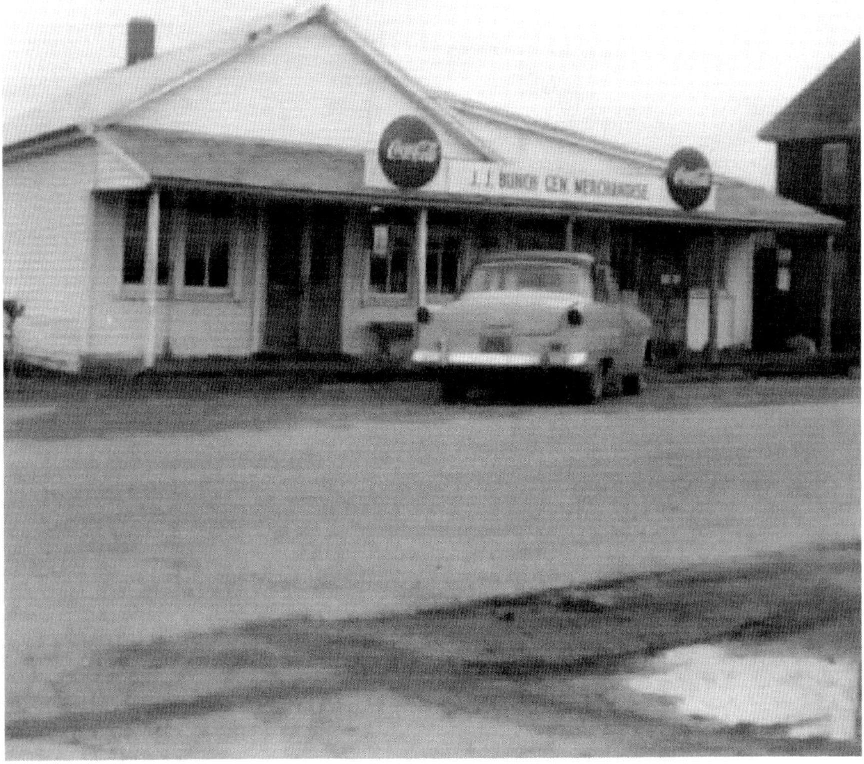


Jerry Bunch's store at Poplar Branch Landing. This is where Currituck, Pine Island and Whalehead Clubs bought their groceries. *Courtesy of Olive Butt.*

the material to the Jones dock in Waterlily and we hauled it across the sound on this barge. Griggs O'Neal, the deputy sheriff in Corolla, had a six-wheel-drive army truck that he hauled it out to the beach on. After that, Jimmy Hayman bought an army truck and we were glad of it. We later used that barge to haul sedge, pine bushes and building material for blinds when I was running Monkey Island Club from 1974 to 1978. So much for the history of that boat.

Mr. John Poyner was superintendent at the Currituck Club from 1909 until 1960, according to his daughter, Mary Glines. My Daddy represented Currituck Club and I can remember Mr. Poyner's daughter, Mary, bringing him up to Daddy's office in the early 1940s to take care of business. He had a green Plymouth or Dodge back then.

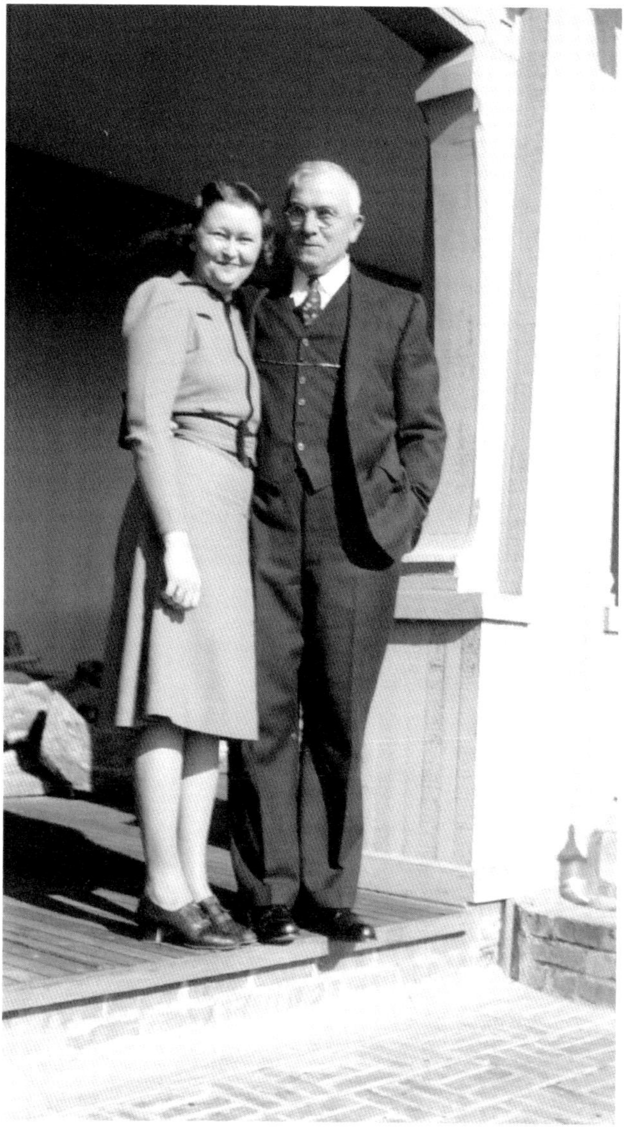

My mother, Edna B. Morris, and Captain Neil Midgett on the porch of the Whalehead Club on December 31, 1940. *Courtesy of the author.*

I talked with Laverne Brickhouse the other day and she told me she started working with Mr. Norman Gregory when she was sixteen years old, and she worked with him for fifteen years. She said when she started work there he had two books. One book was what people owed him and the other was what he owed other people. One day, the IRS man came and told him he needed a better bookkeeping system. After that, he hired Mr. Edward T. Caton, a CPA from Virginia, to set up a set of books for him. He taught Laverne how to use debit and credit bookkeeping.

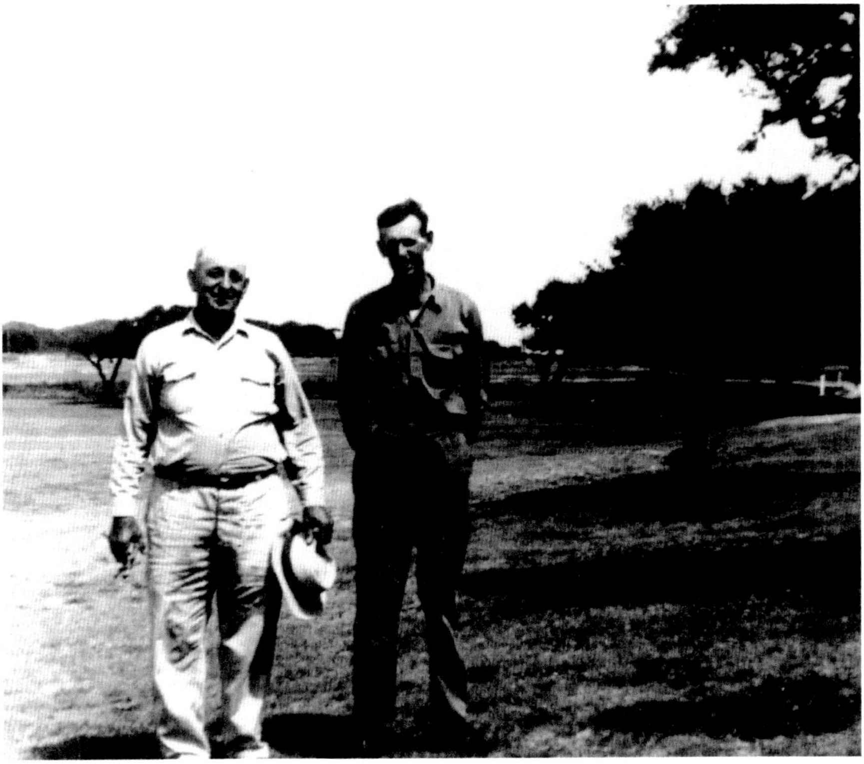

Dexter Snow (left) and Joe Simons on the grounds of the Whalehead Club. *Courtesy of the author.*

Laverne said one day she told Mr. Norman he needed to go collect some money. She said he went to Duck. When he came back, she asked him how he made out. He said, "Well, this old man was a fisherman and he wasn't able to work and his wife was down sick in the bed. I wound up giving him money." Laverne said that's the type of person Mr. Norman Gregory was.

There were a lot of haul seine fishing rigs that fished out of Poplar Branch at this time. Mr. Norman bought fish that mostly ended up in the Fulton Fish Market in New York City. That same market is there today. I see Wanchese Fish Company, Moon Tillett and Willie Etheridge trucks go by here nearly every day at certain times of the year and I know a lot of them are going to Fulton Fish Market.

The carp had to be alive to sell them. The only market for them was the Jewish population in New York and they had to be alive for the rabbi to stab them for them to be holy, so they said. In order to keep the carp alive, the fishermen had what they called a "carp car." This was a skiff that was decked over on the top with a lid on both ends to get the fish in and out. The

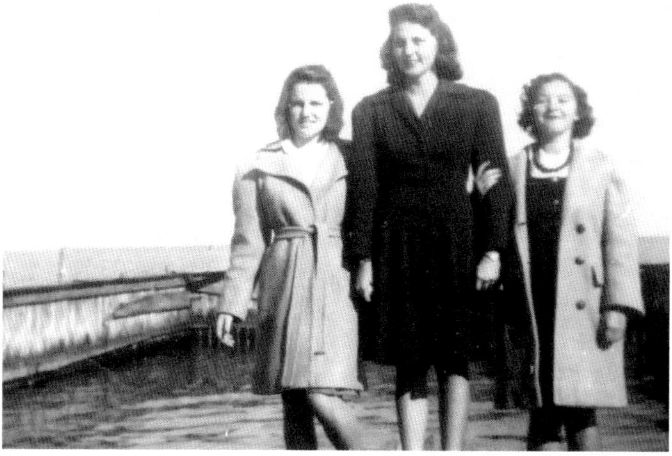

*Left to right:* Laverne Baum, Joyce Baum and Norma Jean Walker at the carp pen at Poplar Branch Landing. *Courtesy of Laverne Baum Brickhouse.*

skiff was bored full of holes so it would stay full of water. The fishermen would tow this and, when they pulled the net in, they would put the carp in the carp car. When they got back to the landing that evening, there was a ramp to pull the carp car up so the water could run out the holes and you could catch the carp, put them in a fish box, weigh them and then dump them in the carp pound. This was a lot of work. I know because I've done it. I fished one winter with Mr. Wallace Davis and Bill Snowden. We fished one of Archie Midgett's rigs out of Waterlily and sold to Mr. Casey Jones. A carp pound was a diked-in area so the carp couldn't get out. Mr. Norman, or whoever the fish buyer might be, would pay the fisherman by the weight before the carp was dumped in the pound. When the tank truck came from New York to pick up the carp, men would get in the pen with a net, catch the carp and load them in the tank truck for the trip to New York. Now you know what fishermen had to go through to catch the lowest-priced fish you could catch, but there were a lot of them and they weighed heavy. Some would weigh forty pounds. According to Laverne, this pen was not only used for carp. She said it had a good, hard, sandy bottom and in the summertime when all the carp had been taken out, all the kids around used it for a swimming pool. She said kids even came from as far as Coinjock to swim there.

Mr. Norman bought into the New Fowler Store in Elizabeth City in about the early 1950s. At this time, Mr. Otto Bateman, who had worked for Mr. Norman for many years, took over the operation at Poplar Branch Landing. They called it Gregory and Bateman. This lasted a few years and then he sold out to Southern Fish Company and Nunemaker's at the beach. Laverne said when Mr. Norman went to Elizabeth City, she went there too.

Laverne also told me that before her time there was a dance hall built out over the water at Poplar Branch Landing called the Blue Moon. Poplar Branch Landing became the lively spot in town. The activity was around the Blue Moon, which was operated by Webb Jones.

# Tilman Merrell

I went to visit Mr. Tilman on October 11, 2007. It was a beautiful fall day. Mr. Tilman is ninety-nine years old and his wife, Miss Elsie, is ninety-five. I had called on Monday and talked to Sandy Royal, one of the ladies who stays with them, and made an appointment to visit him Thursday at 1:00 p.m.

When I arrived, Sandy told me that the nurse, Sonya Gallop, was there. I said, "I'll leave and come back another day."

"Oh, no. Go in and speak to him anyway." When I went in, he kinda' laughed, shook hands with me and said he was glad to see me. Sonya was taking Miss Elsie's blood pressure. I said, "I'll come back another day." Sonya said, "No, please stay and talk to him. This is the most I've ever seen him talk and laugh. It's good for him."

The bottom line here is that duck hunters, even if they're ninety-nine years old, still like to talk about ducks. It brings back fond memories.

Mr. Tilman told me he had started hunting with his daddy, Isaac Merrell, when he was a little boy. He said his daddy raised live geese and ducks for live decoys. "So you've hunted over live decoys?" I asked. "Oh, yes," he said. Miss Elsie spoke up about that time and said she used to go hunting with her daddy. Her daddy was Elle Saunders, who was a well-known guide and made canvas duck and goose decoys. He made them for many of the guides around Poplar Branch Landing. He had a son, Ralph Saunders, who was clerk of court in Currituck for many years. He's

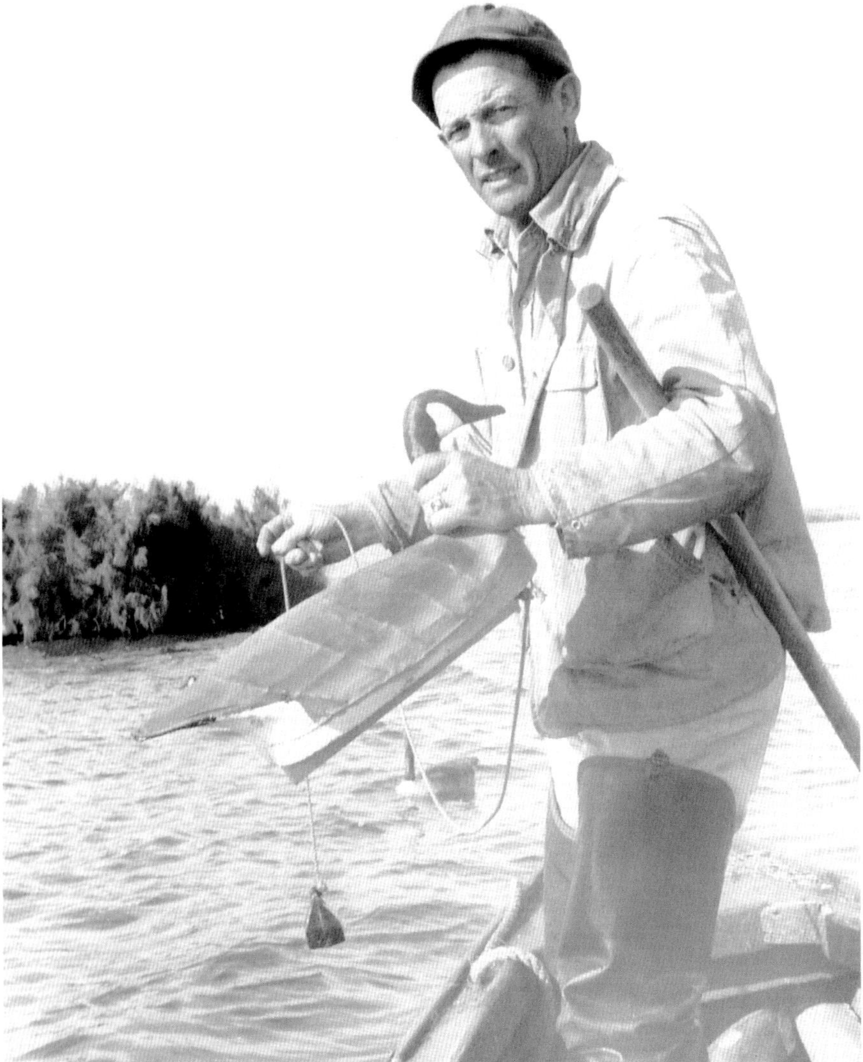

Tilman Merrell tying out goose decoys. *Courtesy of the Merrell family.*

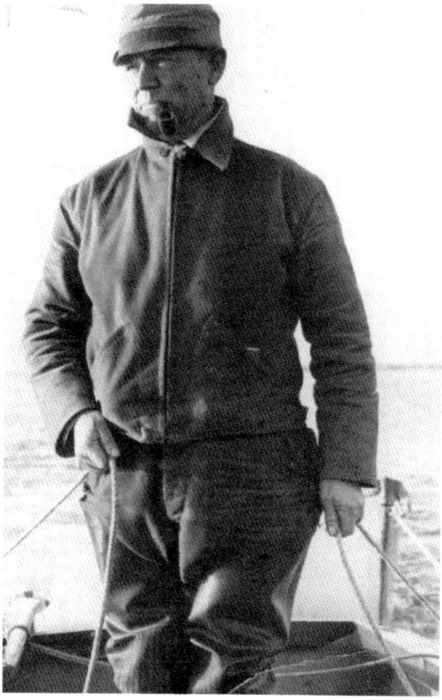

Elle Saunders running a gas boat when he was a young man. Note that he was steering with lines tied to the tiller. *Courtesy of the Merrell family.*

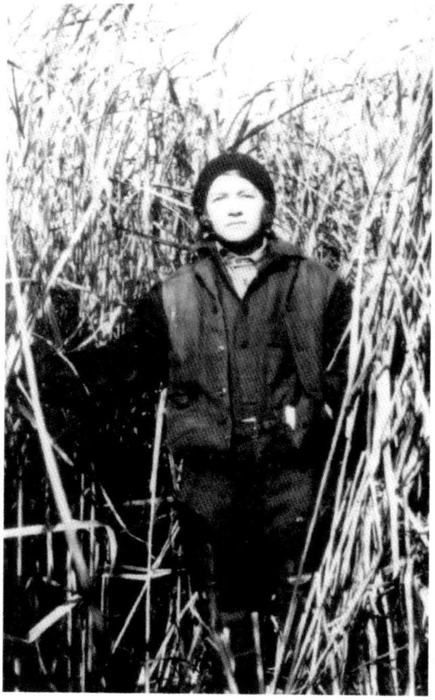

Elsie Saunders (later Elsie Saunders Merrell) hunting in the marsh with her daddy, Elle Saunders. *Courtesy of the Merrell family.*

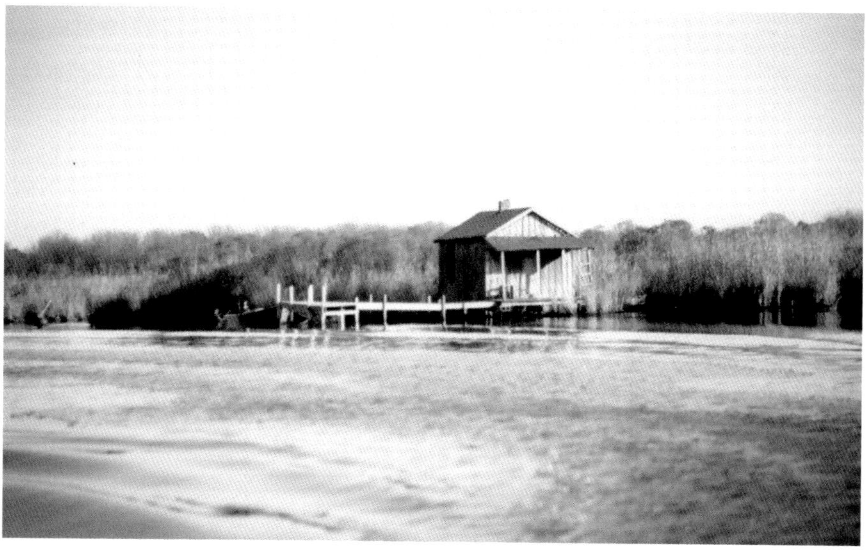

The Currituck Club Guard Camp at Saunders Creek where Tilman Merrell was a marsh guard for seven years. *Courtesy of the Merrell family.*

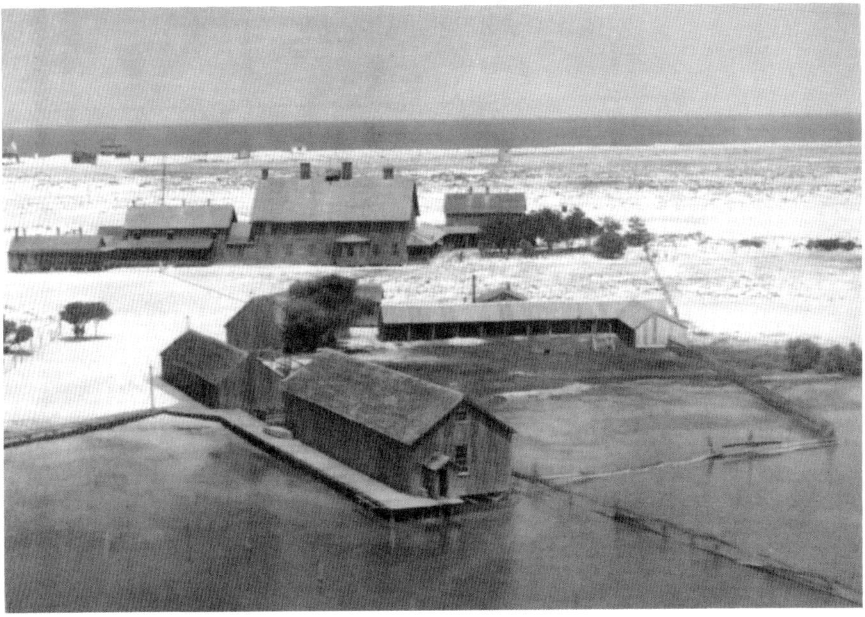

Currituck Shooting Club. *Courtesy of the author.*

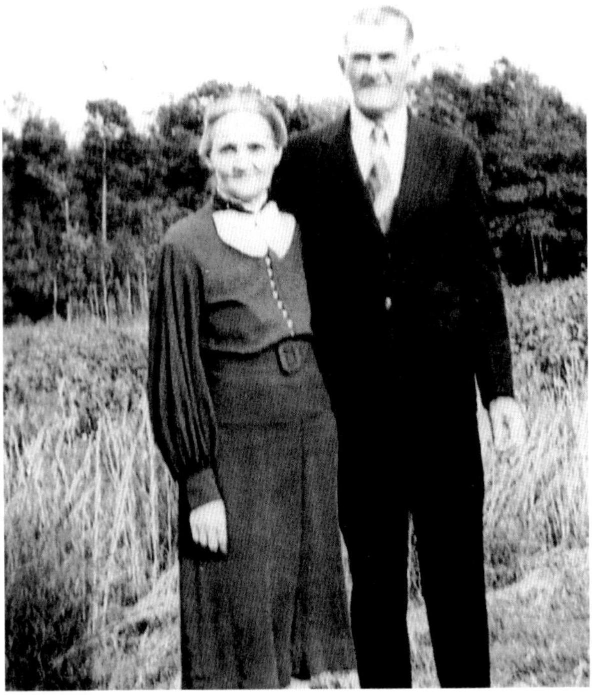

Tilman Merrell's parents, Holly and Isaac. *Courtesy of the Merrell family.*

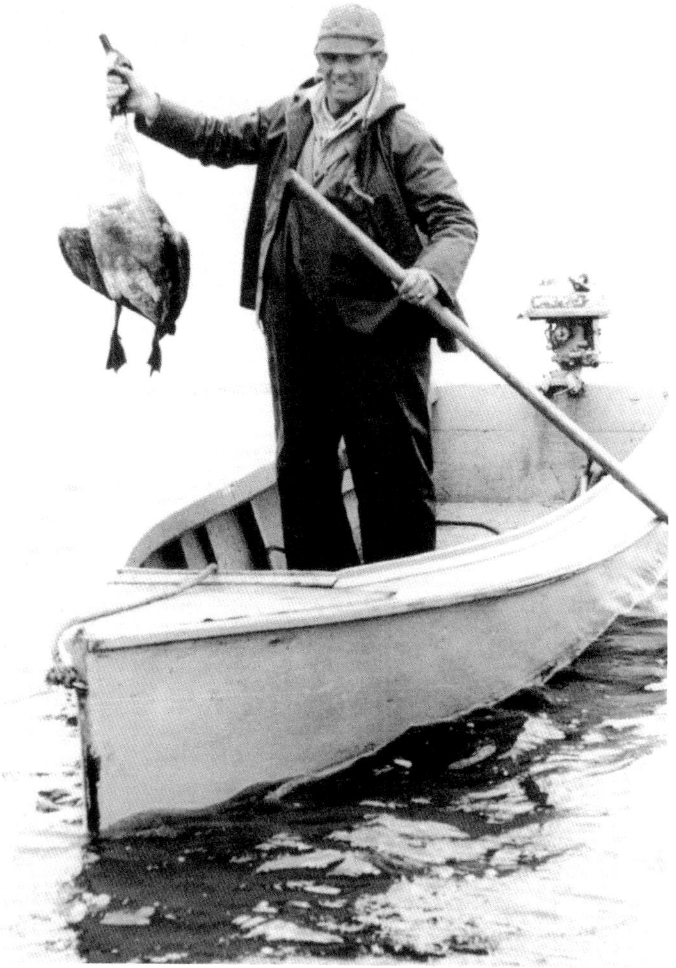

Tilman Merrell. *Courtesy of the Merrell family.*

already been mentioned in one story in this book. Another son, Blanton, was a guide and deputy sheriff in Currituck. Blanton also made canvas decoys, built boats and shaped shoving poles.

Miss Elsie said her daddy's gas boat had a spray hood on her and you could step right out of the boat on to the marsh where his blind was. She said when she and Mr. Tilman got married, she told him she wanted to go hunting with him. She said she thought it was going to be like her daddy's blind, but it wasn't. His was an open-water blind. She said you had to stay in the boat and that boat was just a rocking. She told him to take her ashore and he'd never be bothered with her anymore, and she said he wasn't.

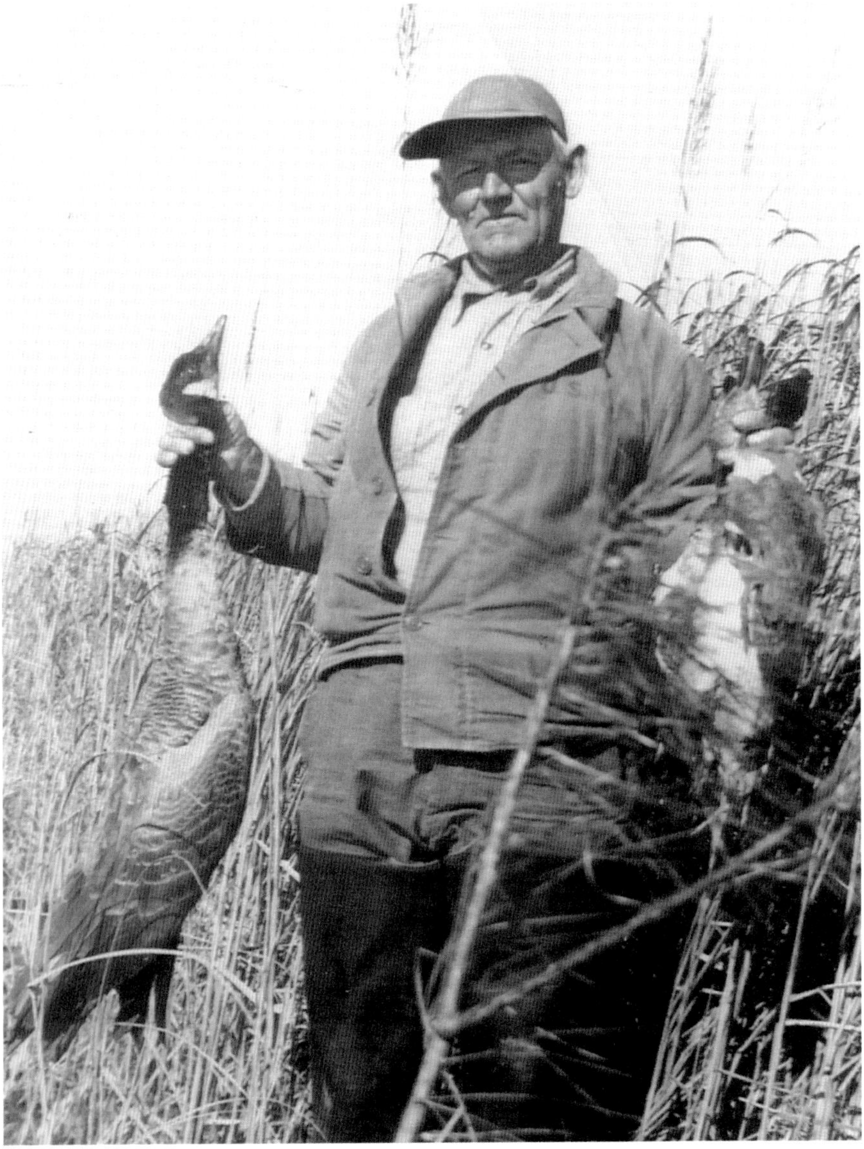

Elle Saunders in later years holding up a goose and ducks. *Courtesy of the Merrell family.*

Mr. Tilman told me at one time or another he worked for Narrows Island Club, Pine Island Club, Dews Island Club and Currituck Club. He told me he guarded the marsh at Currituck Club for seven years. He stayed at the guardhouse in Sanders Creek. I asked him if he ever had any trouble with poachers. He said not that he knew of.

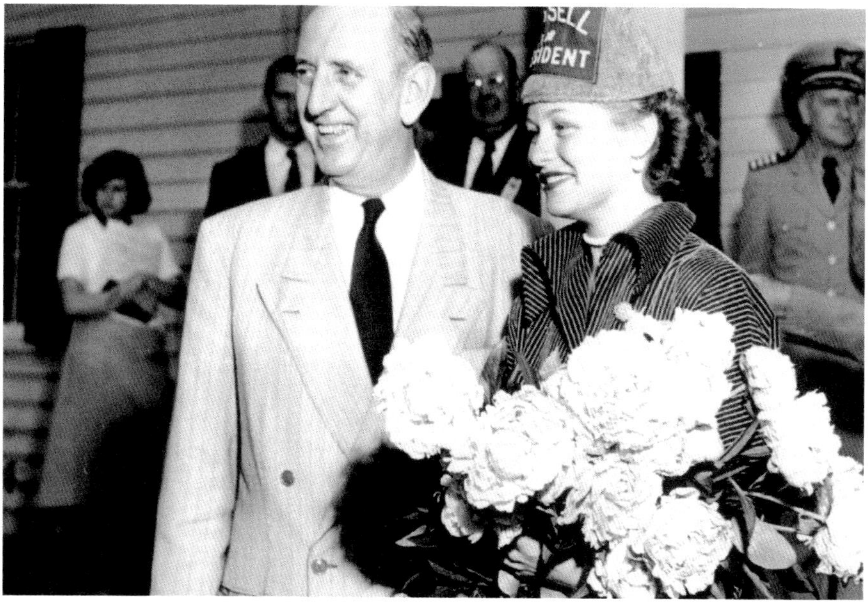

Senator Richard Russell of Georgia—who was running for president of the United States at the time—and Tilman and Elsie Merrell's daughter, Jeanette. She was Miss Currituck at the Potato Festival in Elizabeth City, North Carolina, in 1962. *Courtesy of the Merrell family.*

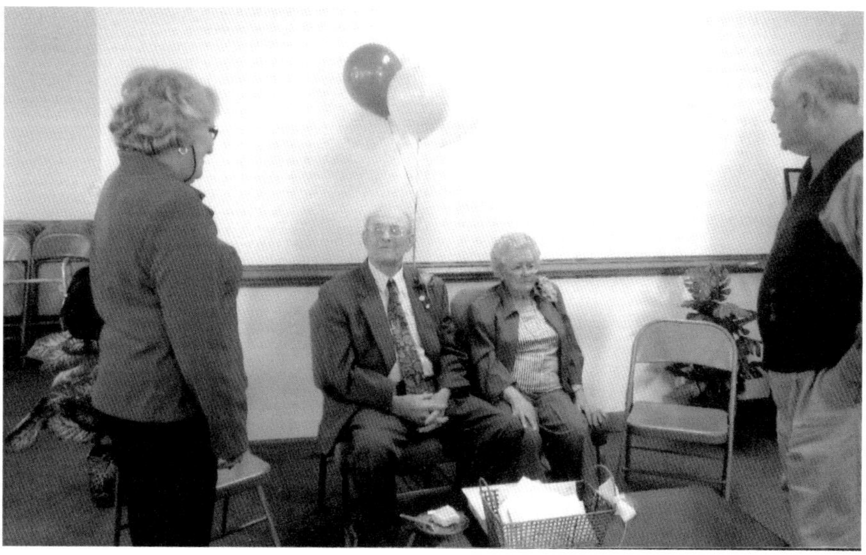

Tilman and Elsie Merrell at their seventy-fifth wedding anniversary. Standing are Jane and John Hawkins. *Courtesy of the Merrell family.*

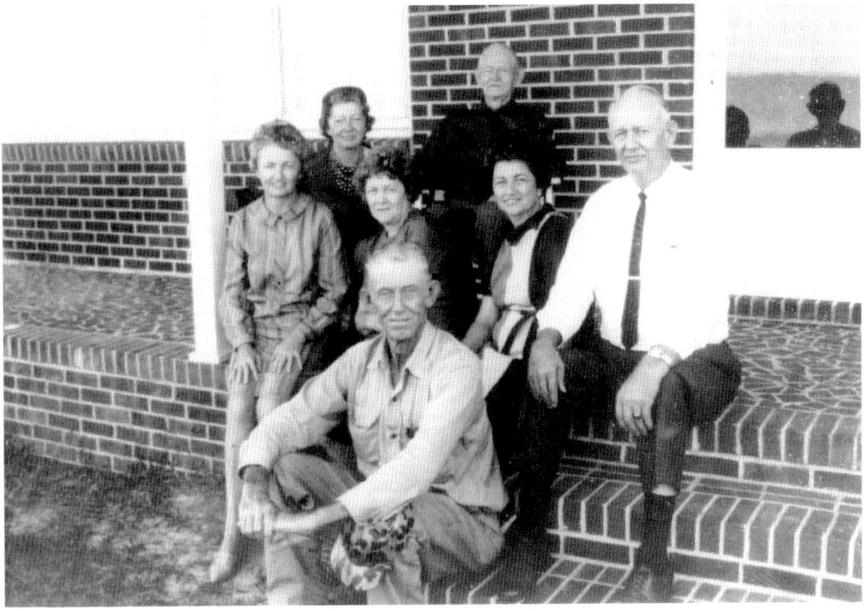

The Saunders family. Sitting in front is Blanton. Bertie and Elle are in the top row. In the middle are Norma, Elsie, Hazel and Ralph. There was one boy, Mervin, who was not in the picture. Ralph was clerk of court for many years. Norma married Ralph Barco. Blanton was a well-known guide in Currituck. He also made decoys, boats and shoving poles, and he was a deputy sheriff. He had an old four-door Plymouth. Although I never saw it myself, I remember folks saying he had an eye ring like you put in the bow of a boat on the floor of the back seat of that Plymouth so he could handcuff his prisoners to it if they were bad. *Courtesy of the Merrell family.*

To save confusion, Currituck Gunning and Fishing Club was on Knotts Island. Currituck Shooting Club, known just as Currituck Club, is said to be the oldest duck club in continuous operation in America. It started in 1857. It is located at Poyner's Hill directly across the Currituck Sound from Poplar Branch Landing. The club burned to the ground in 2002, but the organization is still in operation. The developments of Ocean Sands and Currituck Club were on Currituck Shooting Club property. The club still owns about fifteen hundred acres of marsh.

I told him that Vernon Lee Creekmore (one of the Roving Hunters in my first book) told me "you are the best goose caller he's ever heard." Mr. Tilman said one time he was hunting in the sound in a blind that was his daddy's (Isaac's) when a bunch of geese came over. It was late in the afternoon and those geese knew where they were going. He said most folks honk, but he cackles. He said he started cackling to those geese and the old gander broke off and came right to him. Mr. Jerry Bunch owned a store at

Poplar Branch Landing at the time. He was hunting in the blind right next to him and saw all this take place. That night, Mr. Tilman went to the store and Mr. Jerry said, "Tilman, you beat all I've ever seen. Those geese knew right where they were going for the night and you changed their mind and brought 'em right in to you."

Outside of working at the clubs, Mr. Tilman worked at the blimp base in Elizabeth City during World War II. He and Miss Elsie raised three children: Jeanette, who is the oldest; Wayne, who worked at the Ford plant in Norfolk; and Dan, who is an attorney in Kitty Hawk. Jeanette was a very pretty girl and won Miss Currituck in the Potato Festival in 1962 in Elizabeth City.

Mr. Tilman died since I started writing this book. He was buried on his hundredth birthday, April 3, 2008. He and my mother, Edna Boswood Morris, were both born April 3, 1908, and both went to Poplar Branch School.

# Rovers Fishing in the Ocean

If you read my first book, there was a chapter on the Roving Hunters. They were Baxter Williams, Vernon Lee Creekmore, Fred Newbern, Gordon Sawyer and me. We used my float rig with my gas boat *Rhonda*. We hunted wherever the ducks were, from Ferebee Island in the north end of Currituck Sound to the sound bridge at Point Harbor.

Now for the Roving Fishermen. Vernon Lee had two cottages in Kitty Hawk in the 1960s. He rented out one in the summer and used the other one himself. Now mind you, these were not modern-day cottages like you think about today. As an example, the hot water was a thirty-gallon tank on the roof heated by the sun.

We had many fishing trips out of Oregon Inlet and stayed at this cottage, but I'm only going to tell you about one. These trips were mostly in the 1960s. Vernon Lee had an old gas boat about twenty-five feet long that Mr. Wilton Walker had built for the Tice brothers. Vernon Lee kept this boat at the Oregon Inlet Fishing Center.

On this particular trip, it was Baxter, Vernon Lee, Fred and me. We got down to Kitty Hawk to the cottage late one Friday afternoon. As night came on, we were getting hungry so we decided we would go out on the town and see what we could find. We ended up at the Drafty Tavern on the causeway to Manteo. This was about where Pirates Cove Marina is now. Well, when we got in there, who did we run into but Walton Carter and H.D. Newbern Jr. (this was before either of them was married). To put it mildly, they were

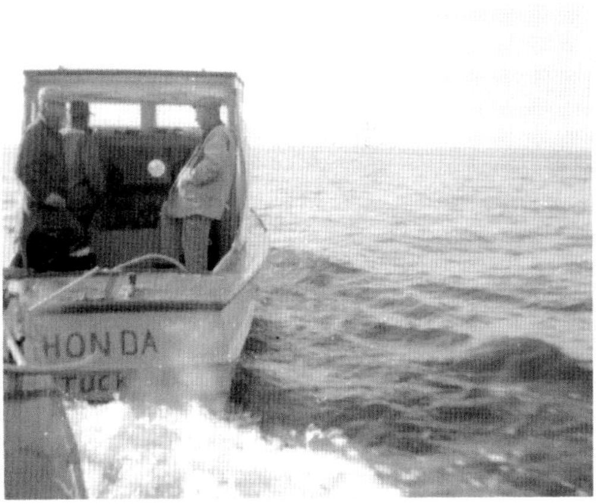

*Left to right:* Baxter Williams, Vernon Lee Creekmore and Fred Newbern. The boat (*Rhonda*) is mine, and she is very similar to Vernon Lee's. *Courtesy of the author.*

feeling no pain. We were all at the same table and I was afraid we were going to get thrown out of there. When you get thrown out of the Drafty Tavern, that's bad! As soon as we had got our "sumpin' to eat" I told our crew, "Let's get out of here before we get in jail"—and we did.

The next morning we were up early. We had breakfast at Sam and Omie's in Nags Head. Then we went on to Oregon Inlet Fishing Center. We loaded our gear in the boat. Vernon Lee checked the oil in the old flat head V8 Ford and then got it cranked up. We didn't dare cut it off until we got back because we were scared it wouldn't start.

We went on out the inlet and couldn't find the blues. We kept going out until we were out of sight of land. Now think about this. We didn't have a radio or any kind of communication. No electronics. The only thing we had was a compass, plus an engine we were afraid to cut off to check the oil. When I look back on it, I think we must have been crazy. We were trolling along and we weren't catching anything. I fell asleep. Fred got hold of my line and pulled it in and tied a Pepsi Cola bottle on it. Fred always took a case of Pepsi Colas when we were going hunting or fishing. That's when they were in wooden crates and glass bottles. He eased the bottle back overboard, and when that thing came taut on my line it liked to have jerked the pole out of my hand. Now the rest of those boys were making out like I had a big fish on. When I got that thing in, I had some nice words for them that the publisher couldn't print here.

This is not the end of the story. We got back in close to the breakers and found the bluefish. We were catching them two at a time. We stopped when we got 125!

I'm sorry to say that everybody but me in this story has passed on to the Great Beyond. I don't know how much time I have left. That's why I'm trying to write these stories for the generations to come.

# Famous People

One of the people the author has had the pleasure of meeting on the waters of Currituck Sound is Walter Cronkite, who at the time was said to be the most respected man in America.

One day in the 1970s, my son Walton and I were taking a lady out to see Long Point Island, which I had for sale. This is a sixty-acre island about two or three miles north of Coinjock Bridge. We were in Walt's sixteen-foot skiff with a fifty-horsepower Mercury outboard motor.

When we were going back, this sailboat had run aground. This was nothing unusual. Sailboats are always running aground along that part of the Intracoastal Waterway (ICW). If you get out of the channel, the water is only about three or four feet deep. We went up to this boat to see if we could help. The man onboard gave us a line, but that little outboard wouldn't budge him. Then we took an anchor out to deeper water and brought the line back for him to hook on to his winch while we took a line from his mast and tried to heel the boat over. That didn't work either. I had a gas boat (inboard motorboat), but she was all the way on the other side of Churches Island at Waterlily. I told him he'd just have to call the Coast Guard. They had a station at Coinjock then and would come help him. Now they won't come unless you are in danger of losing your life. He didn't want to call the Coast Guard, but I told him I'd done all I could do for him and I left.

Soon after we left, my son said, "Daddy, that was Walter Cronkite." The lady with us said, "Yes, it was." That's why he didn't want to call the Coast Guard.

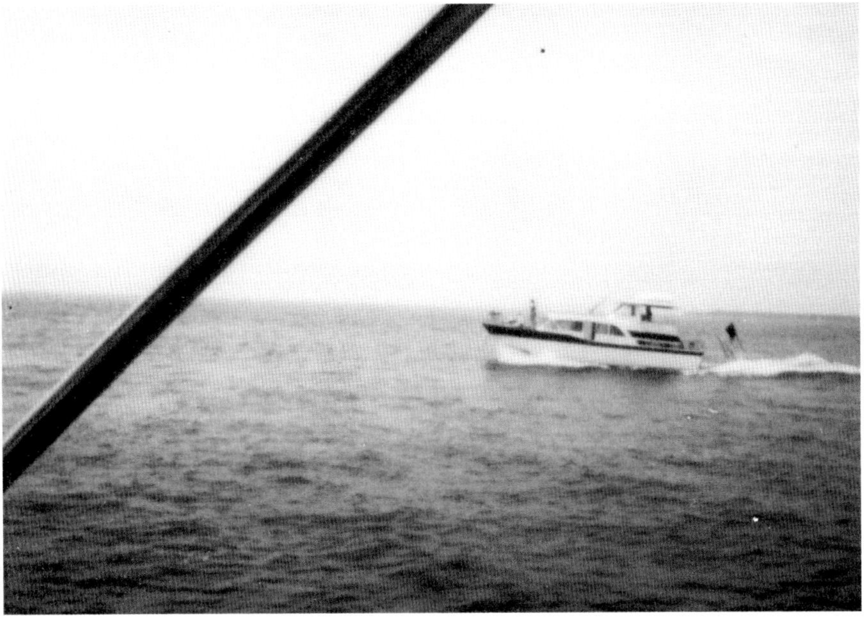

*Miss Bessie,* owned by William and Gaston Small from Weeksville, North Carolina, leading the fleet to Manteo for the 400th anniversary, with Walter Cronkite aboard as the grand marshal. This was in 1984. *Courtesy of the author.*

When I got home, I wrote him a letter and told him I was sorry I didn't recognize him even though I did watch him on the news every night. I just wasn't expecting to see him in Coinjock Bay. In a few days, I got a nice letter from him. I lost that letter when my office burned in 1980.

A few years later, when they had the 400th anniversary of the Lost Colony, they were going to have a parade of boats from Elizabeth City to Manteo. Walter Cronkite had agreed to be the grand marshal. He was to ride on *Miss Bessie,* a forty-two-foot Chris-Craft that William and Gaston Small owned. I was to be in the parade with the *Frances M,* my forty-foot Owens. The night before the parade, there was a cocktail party in Elizabeth City for the people in the parade. I introduced myself to Walter Cronkite and he remembered the incident. We had a nice conversation. You never know who you will meet on the waters of Currituck.

Another person I met was Malcolm Forbes, who owned *Forbes* magazine and many other companies. He had one of the largest yachts that used to come through Coinjock in the late 1970s. He later had one built that was too big to come through the ICW. He named all his yachts the *Highlander.* He always stayed at Harrison's Marina, which is on the opposite side of the canal from where I owned a lot and dock. At the time, I had an old thirty-five-foot wood Pacemaker. He wanted to take a picture of his boat. Eddie Harrison saw me on my boat so he brought Mr. Forbes over and introduced him to me. I invited him aboard and he took a picture of his boat. Another example that you never know who you'll meet on the waters of Currituck.

You would be surprised at the people that come down the ICW and stop at Coinjock. The marinas are very discreet about who is tied up where because they have to protect their customers' privacy. At Piney Island Club, there is an osprey nest at the end of the dock. The ICW is just about one hundred feet west of this dock. One day, Jimmy Dean's yacht, *Big Bad John*, was passing and Jimmy Markert, the caretaker, got a picture of the osprey on the nest with *Big Bad John* in the background.

# Charlie Dozier and G.C. Sawyer

Charlie Dozier and Lawrence Dozier Jr. were farmers in Jarvisburg, North Carolina, as was their daddy, Mr. Lawrence Sr. He was also sheriff in Currituck County for many years. Mr. Lawrence was uncle to my mother-in-law, Birdye Dozier Meiggs Beasley. Lawrence Jr. was kind of quiet, but Charlie was always laughing and full of fun. Charlie loved to hunt ducks and geese. The only problem was that if there was only one duck left in the world, I think Charlie would have shot him.

G.C. Sawyer was Charlie Dozier's brother-in-law, neighbor and good friend. His daddy, Mr. Grover Sawyer, had run a hunting lodge at Hog Quarter Landing from way back in the days of battery hunting.

The main highway through Currituck County is U.S. 158. There is a road in Jarvisburg called Jarvisburg Road that turns off east of 158 and parallels it for a ways before it joins the main road again. At the time of this story, this road was dirt. The Doziers owned land on both sides of that road. They had dug a canal from Dews Quarter Bay up to the high land on their farm on the east side of this road where they dug out a boat basin and built a boathouse.

At this time, there were a lot of geese in the cornfield right back of Charlie's house on 158. On this particular day, it was raining. Geese like to go in the field to feed in this type of weather. Now there is another important player in this story. Remember me telling you about Mr. Albert Sumrell building the boat for Mr. Adams? Well, now, Mr. Sumrell was a federal game warden and lived just a little farther down the road. It was always a cat-and-mouse game with Charlie and Mr. Albert.

Charlie and G.C. were both in a big ditch. They both had foul-weather gear on. They were not right next to each other. They had already killed over their limit of geese, so G.C. started toward Charlie and Charlie thought he was Mr. Albert, so he started running. G.C. thought Charlie had seen Mr. Albert. They chased each other all the way down that ditch, across the dirt road and down to the boathouse. They were going to jump in the boat and haul buggy. When they got there, both of their tongues were hanging out. It was only then that they found out they had been chasing each other. It was just a miracle they didn't die of heart attacks. I wish I could tell that story just half as good as Charlie told it to me many years ago.

Charlie and John Jr. Wright were good friends during the summertime. They would sit around Jack Helms's store and spin yarns, but when hunting season came, they were dire enemies. I'll give you one or two examples.

John Jr. was superintendent of Dews Island Club for the Chathams and later the Haneses bought into it. Deep Creek, which goes west of Dews Island, joins Dews Quarter Bay with Currituck Sound and separates Dews Island from the mainland. At the closest point, it is only about one hundred feet wide. The clubhouse is on the east side of Dews Island. The only legal access to this island is by boat. When Mr. Thurman Chatham bought Dews Island, he hired John Wright Jr. as superintendent and worked a deal with John Jr. to have access through the Wright's farm to Deep Creek, but John Jr. would not sell the access. *That* is called job security. Now Mr. Chatham was going to build a humpback bridge across Deep Creek, meaning it would be high enough in the center for small boats to get under. Charlie found out about this and said the bridge was not high enough for the cabin of his gas boat to get under when the tide was high. He put a windshield on the back of the cabin to make it higher.

Charlie even complained to the Army Corps of Engineers and made John Jr. put a draw in the bridge. It was rigged up with a block and tackle so you could raise it up. Charlie didn't need to go through Deep Creek and didn't much; he was usually going across the sound or on the east side of Dews Island. He just did it to aggravate John Jr.

John Jr. always fed the ducks off the end of the dock so the sportsmen could see them from the clubhouse. Charlie loved to run those ducks up just to aggravate John Jr. I was friends with both Charlie and John Jr. I hauled potatoes for both of them in the summertime. I also bought potatoes from both of them for a man in New York. Charlie had a kind of speedboat with a big outboard on it. One day I was riding with him and he decided he was going to run those ducks up. I didn't want John Jr. to see

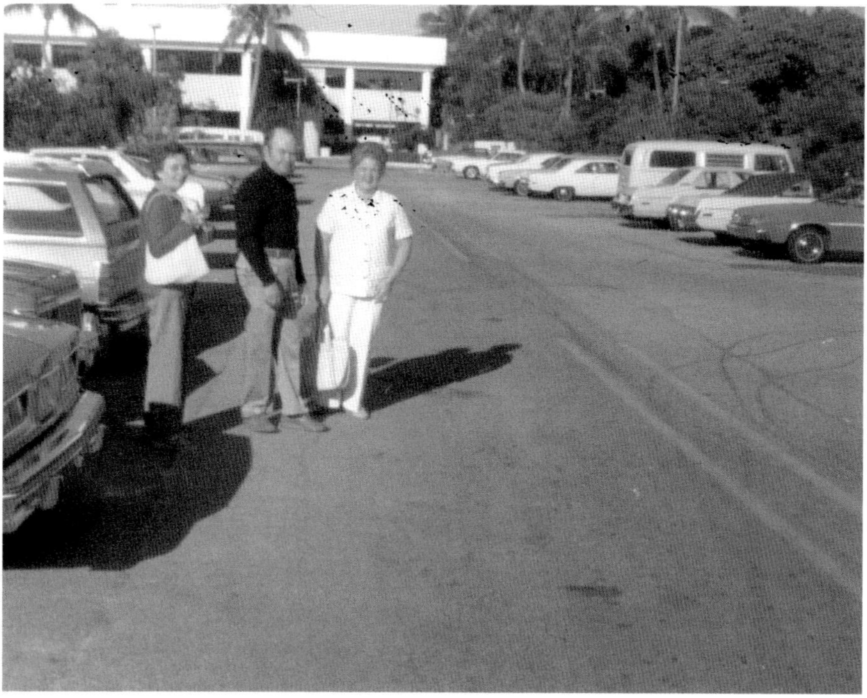

*Left to right:* Doris and Charlie Dozier and Frances Morris in the Bahamas in 1978. *Courtesy of the author.*

me in there with him. I bent my head down and hid my face. Charlie ran up there wide open and spun her around almost hitting the dock. Ducks were taking off in a high state of alarm. There could be a book written on the feud between these two during hunting season. It was like the Hatfields and the McCoys.

While I'm talking about that little speedboat of Charlie Dozier's, there is another story about it. One day Fred Newbern, Robert Balance, Vernon Lee Creekmore, Baxter Williams and I had my float box tied out just north of Dews Island. We were shooting canvasbacks and we had too many. I had a dozen new decoy weights I had just bought from Sanders Company in Elizabeth City. They came wired together and they were still on the wire. They were in the cabin of my gas boat, *Rhonda*.

We left Robert Balance in the gas boat and the rest of us got in the skiff to take up the decoys. We had tied the extra canvasbacks to those weights. Fred told Robert if he turned his cap around to drop the canvasbacks overboard. We saw this speedboat coming around the north end of Dews Island just a flying. We just knew that was the game warden. Fred started spinning his cap around and Robert dropped the canvasbacks overboard. The boat came up to us and it was Charlie Dozier. Fred hollered at Robert and said, "Did you throw those ducks overboard?"

"You said if you turned your cap around to drop them and you were spinning your cap so I thought I better drop them quick." Case closed. There are a dozen duck weights and several canvasback bones on the bottom of Currituck Sound in about ten feet of water just north of Dews Island.

# Woodrow Whitson

I knew Woodrow Whitson most of my life, but for this story I interviewed his daughter and son-in-law, Dot and Bobby Henley, and his son, Wilbert Whitson. What I do know about Woodrow is he could spin yarns nonstop. I think the sportmen came as much to hear his stories as to hunt or fish. His great-grandson, Alex Evans, is a good friend of my grandson, Chet Morris. I used to take them duck hunting. Now they take me. I told Alex as long as he lives, Woodrow Whitson will never die because he never shuts his mouth.

I never knew Woodrow to do anything but work on the water. Dot said he worked at Consolidated Aircraft in Elizabeth City during World War II. As a guide, he started out carrying sportsmen for Miss Bernie and Mr. Russell Griggs at Hampton Lodge (Hampton Lodge is featured in my second book, *Currituck Memories and Adventures)*. As a matter of fact, Woodrow, his brother Cecil and his son Wilbert all guided at Hampton Lodge. Wilbert said that is where he took his first hunting party when he was sixteen years old.

Dot said when Miss Bernie was ready to sell Hampton Lodge she offered it to her daddy for $35,000 and said he could pay for it any way he wanted to. That was a lot of money in the 1940s and Woodrow just didn't see how he could ever pay for it. Incidentally, that same property was on the market in 2006 for $13 million. It hasn't sold as of yet. The property is the very north tip of Churches Island, or Waterlily as it is now called. All the same place. If I recall right, there are about five hundred acres there. About two

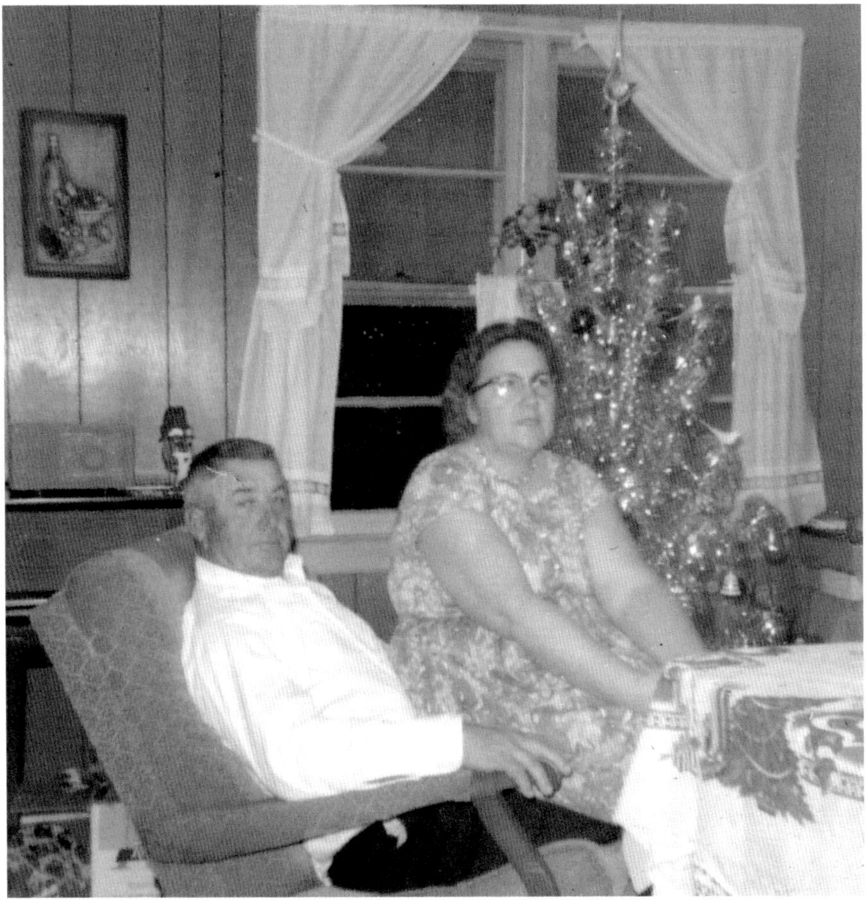

Woodrow and Lillian "Big Mama" Whitson. *Courtesy of Dot Henley.*

hundred acres are usable and the rest is marsh or wetlands. Dot said when her daddy looked back, he could have sold enough muskrat furs off the marsh to have paid for it.

Dot said one Christmas, when she was little, her daddy said they weren't going to have anything for Christmas because he didn't have any money. She said a day or two before Christmas somebody came by and wanted to buy some ducks, and that made their Christmas.

It used to be that hunting violations were not looked on as negatively as they are today. The population of Currituck County was about six thousand. There wasn't much to do here. You farmed, fished, worked in the log woods, drove a produce truck or left and went to work somewhere else. It was a poor county then and hard to stay here and make a living. I know because I stayed here and it wasn't easy in my early adult life.

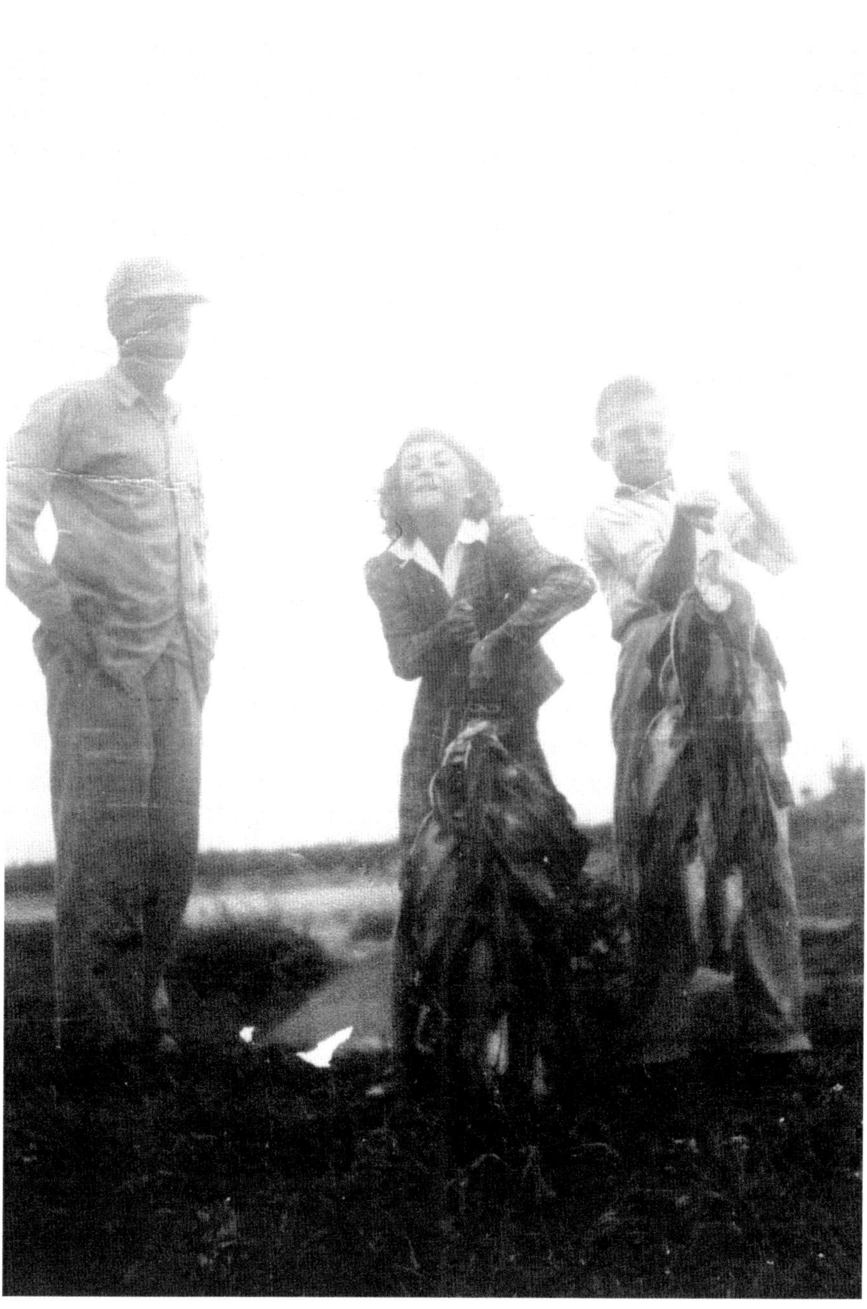

*Left to right:* Woodrow, Dot and Wilbert Whitson with strings of fish. *Courtesy of Dot Henley.*

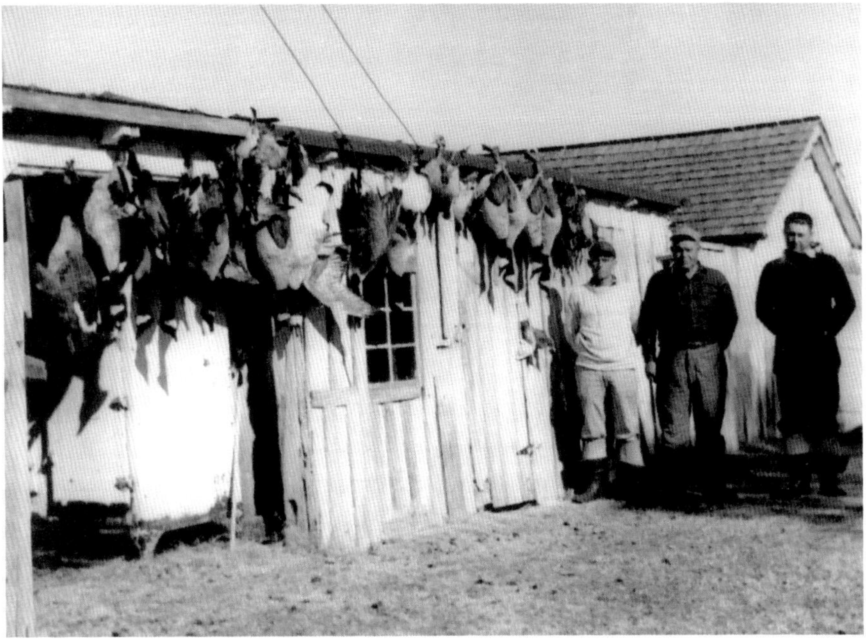

*Left to right:* Wilbert, Cecil and Woodrow Whitson at Hampton Lodge when Wilbert was sixteen years old. *Courtesy of Dot Henley.*

The point I'm trying to make here is that wildfowl was food. Although it was not legal, there were some who bought game and would sell it in Norfolk or up north. The person who comes to my mind as a buyer of game was Charlie Snowden. He bought and sold fish and knew all the local hunters and fishermen in the area. He probably bought game from them as much to help them as to make money for himself. In looking back, Charlie kinda' lived on the edge, but he helped a lot of people in this county.

The fines were not too much for game violations and it was not frowned upon by the community like it is now. Of course, the game wardens were always after somebody for firelighting or some other violation. In stories to come you are going to hear a lot more about this. I wanted to prepare you for it.

Now back to Woodrow. He got started in the guiding business for himself one day in 1946 when he and Wilbert were going home and there were two men fishing on the canal bank. Woodrow stopped and talked to them. They were from Lumberton, North Carolina. One was Jack Price. Dot couldn't remember the other's name. Woodrow told them to "come on home with me and I'll carry you fishing tomorrow." They did and they went back for years. They told other people and word got around. That's how he got

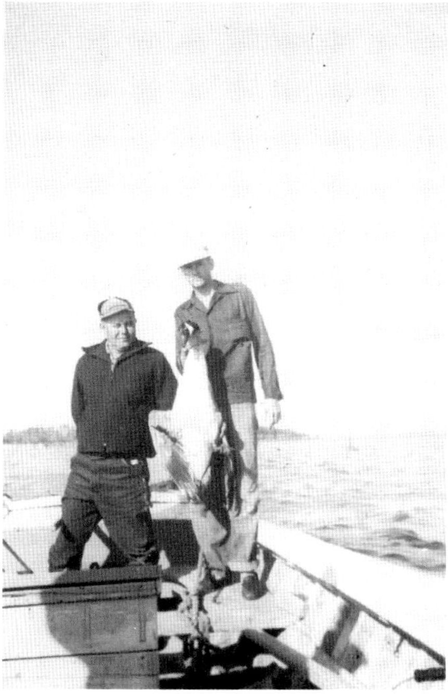

Cecil Whitson, Woodrow's brother, and a sportsman in old Russell Griggs's battery boat that was built in 1927. *Courtesy of Wilbert Whitson.*

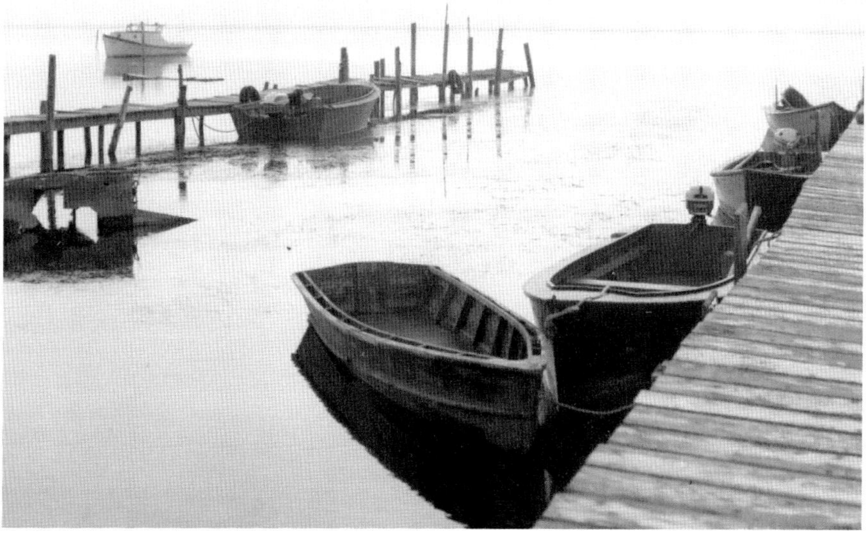

Woodrow Whitson's dock on Churches Island, Waterlily. Russell Griggs's gas boat is tied out to stake. *Courtesy of Dot Henley.*

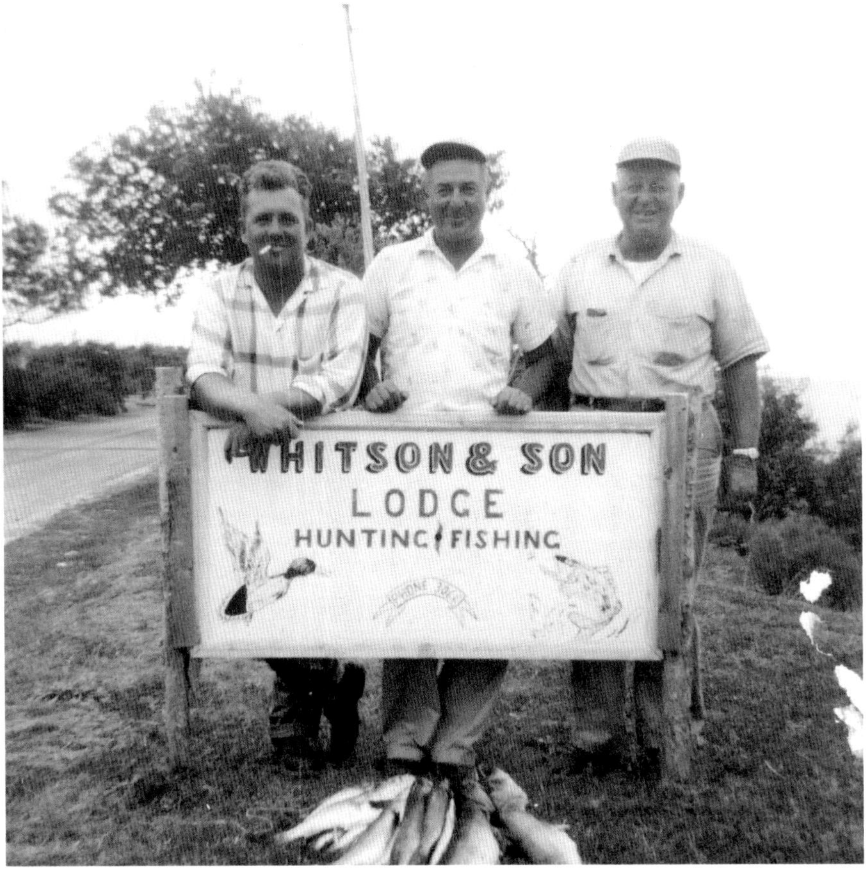


*Left to right:* Wilbert Whitson, Woodrow Whitson and Gilbert Curles. *Courtesy of Dot Henley.*

started. The house he was living in then could only accommodate four extra people. He was in such demand that he needed a larger house so he bought a house from Raynard Collins and added on to it. He named it "Whitson and Son Lodge." Dot said she heard that at one time Mr. Ned Burgess, the famous decoy carver from Churches Island, lived there. She said the most folks they ever had staying there at once was eighteen. I asked who he had guiding for him and she said: Mr. Baum, Gilbert Curles, her granddaddy Roy Craine, her brother Wilbert, her uncle Cecil, Weldon Beasley, Thomas Caroon and her daddy. Sometimes Roland Twiford guided for him, but most of the time Roland guided for Mr. Casey Jones.

We got to talking about Ned Burgess and the different places he lived. Dot, Bobby and I all remembered him. Dot said the only time she was ever in his house, he was in the kitchen whittling out duck heads. She said everything was on the floor: potato peelings, shavings and all.

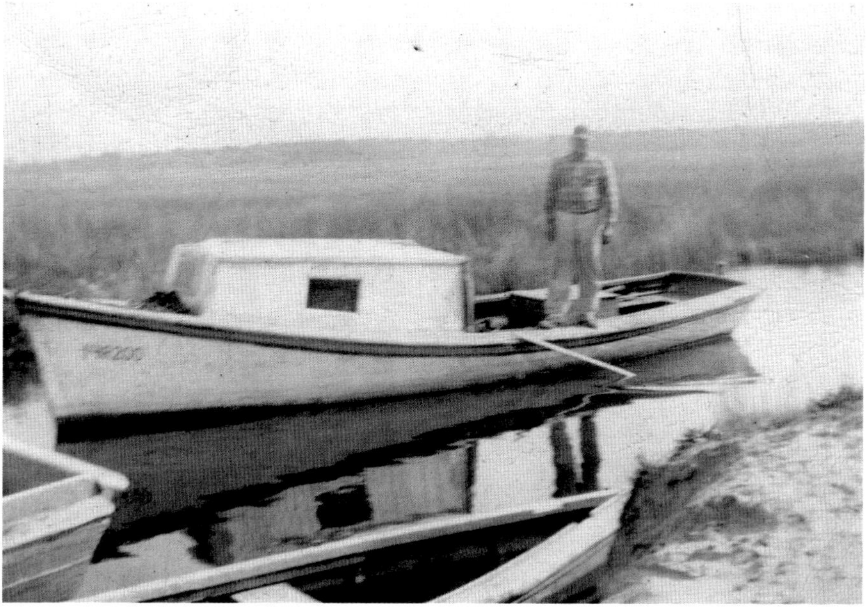

Roy Crain, Woodrow Whitson's father-in-law, in a canal beside the road to Waterlily.
*Courtesy of Wilbert Whitson.*

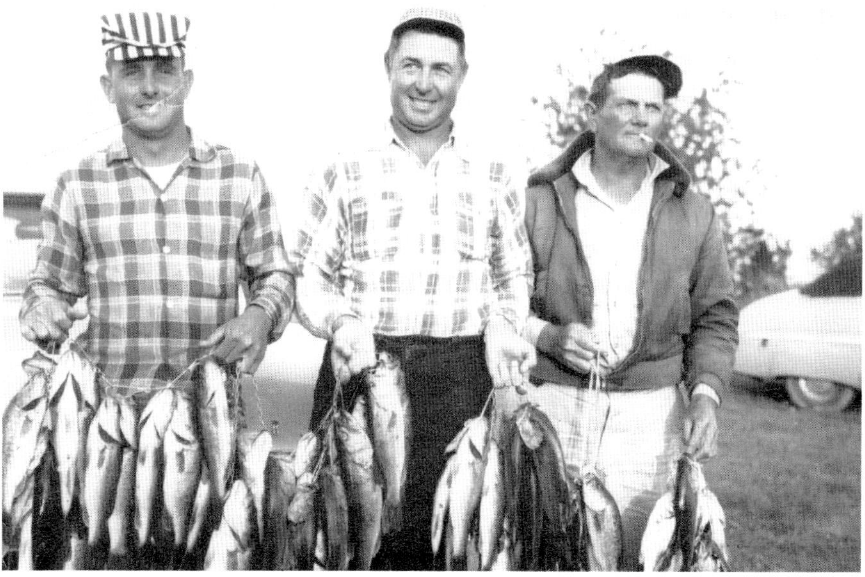

*Left to right:* Wilbert Whitson, Woodrow Whitson and Weldon Beasley with a string of bass.
*Courtesy of Wilbert Whitson.*

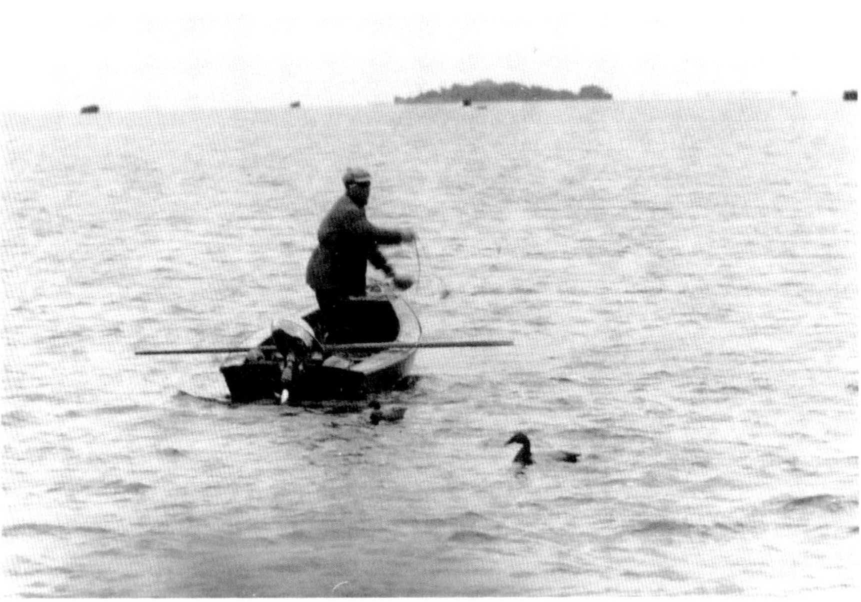

Wilbert Whitson tying out in Currituck Sound with Monkey Island and duck blinds in the background. *Courtesy of Wilbert Whitson.*

Back to Woodrow. He fished mostly with set nets. But Bobby said he did have a haul seine about eight hundred yards long that he used sometimes. He also eeled and did some turtling.

Bobby said in the freeze of 1961, he and Dot walked about halfway across the sound. They took an axe and chopped a hole in the ice and it was about ten inches thick. When the ice broke up, there were icebergs all down the shore. Dot said her daddy's gas boat was tied to the end of his dock and the ice knocked the stern out of the boat and pushed the motor forward.

I told Dot I remembered one time Woodrow was over around Rat Creek across the sound and a storm blew up out of the north and carried the tide out so fast the boat was aground and they had to spend the night out there. Dot said, "Yeah, me, Bobby and Wilbert were with him." She said the headlines in the *Daily Advance* the next day didn't look good. It said "Three Men and a Woman Spent the Night in the Sound." It didn't say it was her daddy, her husband and her brother! She said the wind must have been blowing seventy miles an hour. They all said they had never seen the water go out so fast. The water is shallow there anyway. Before they could get their gear out of the blind and in the skiff, the skiff was setting on bottom. They found a pole they could put under the skiff for a roller. By the time they would get almost to the water, the water would be gone again. They finally got to the gas boat and, of course, she was aground. Wilbert said his

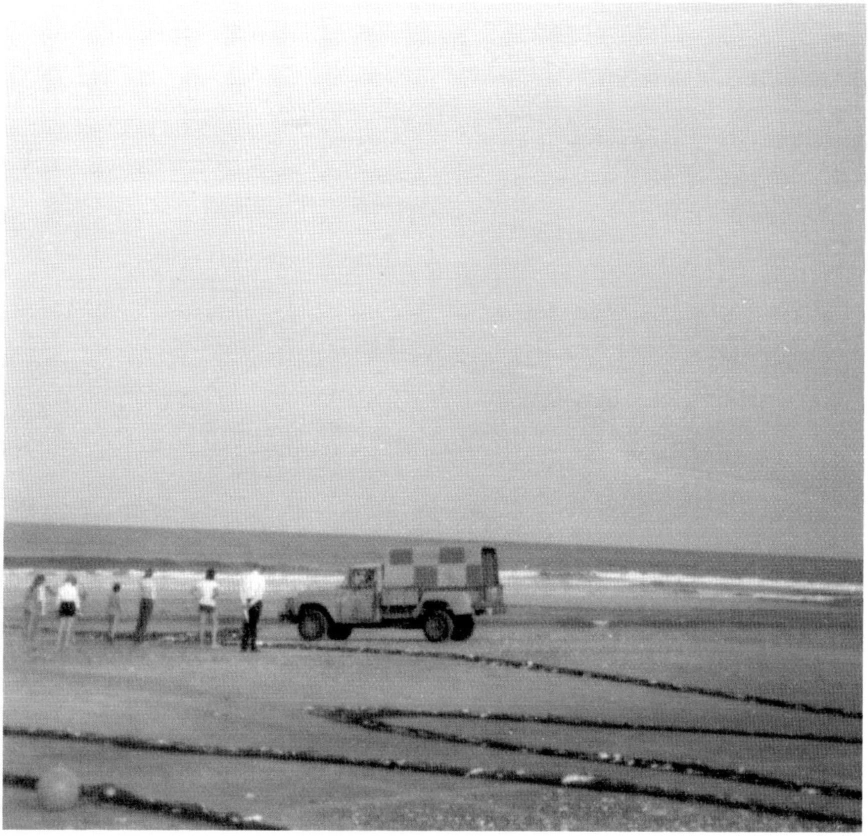

My family, including Mama and Daddy, watching fishermen pull in a net on Currituck Beach in 1972. *Courtesy of the author.*

daddy wanted them to try to get to Monkey Island, but he wouldn't go. He said he didn't believe that sixteen-foot skiff would make it with the four of them in her.

They got in the cabin of the gas boat. Woodrow said, "Don't go to sleep or you'll freeze to death." It wasn't long before they heard him snoring! About four o'clock in the morning, they heard the anchor line rattling the ring in the stem post. They knew she was floating. They got her off and went home, so there was a happy ending. It could have been a sad one if they'd tried to go to Monkey Island in that skiff.

In talking to Wilbert, he said he'd worked all of his life on the water, except for a short time when he worked for Tidewater Construction in Virginia. He mostly fishes with set nets in Currituck Sound, but he fishes some in the ocean off Currituck Beach. In fact, he is getting ready to go to the beach rock fishing this month (December 2007). He said it's hard to fish

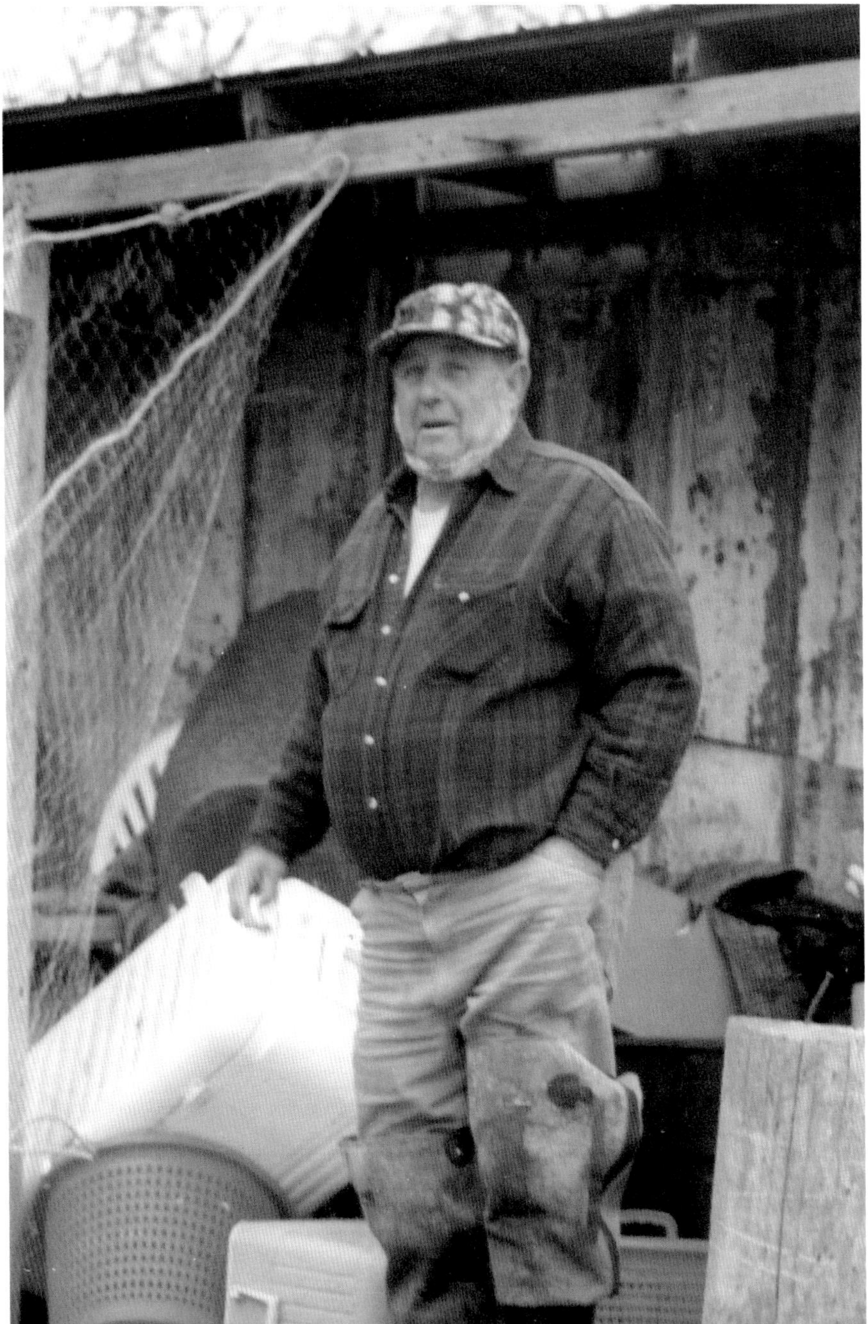

Wilbert Whitson on his dock in front of his landing house on Churches Island. *Courtesy of Wilbert Whitson.*

on the beach now because of so many tourists. Wilbert said the most fish he had ever helped catch on the beach was 354 boxes of spot.

Here's the way they fish on the beach: one end of the net is anchored to the beach and the rest of the net is in the dory. They put the dory to sea and run the net out. When they get to the end of it, they drop an anchor with a line tied to it so they can trip it. They run this line back to the shore against the tide and anchor it on the beach. When they get ready to pull the net in, they hook a vehicle on to this line and when they pull it, the anchor offshore is tripped and they keep pulling until the net is on the beach. I used to have a little net and did this just for fun and to catch fish to eat, but it got to be so many tourists I don't do it anymore.

Wilbert told me about the first time Dr. Shaeffer went to the lodge. He said he was his guide and Dr. Shaeffer killed thirty-three ducks and a goose. That night at the supper table, Dr. Shaeffer said he thought he was going duck hunting. Woodrow told him if he was not satisfied with thirty-three ducks and a goose, then after he finished supper he could pack his bags and get out of there. Wilbert said he changed his tune then. After that, Dr. Shaeffer and Woodrow got to be good friends. I know this because he bought property in Currituck. Years later, when he got ready to sell it, Woodrow introduced me to him and I sold it for him.

# Roland Twiford

I need to give you a little background on the Twifords' connection to Monkey Island so you can better understand the story. Roland's daddy was Mr. George and his mother was Miss Babe Twiford. Mr. George was superintendent of Monkey Island Club from 1928 until 1961. The property was owned by the Penn family from Reidsville, North Carolina. Mr. Charles A. Penn, who was one of the founders of the American Tobacco Company, bought out the other members of the club in 1932, and it was owned by the Penn family until I sold it for them in 1974. They had to take it back, and I sold it again in 1978. The property consisted of Monkey Island itself, which was seven acres; Mary Island, which was marsh; and three miles of Currituck Beach and marsh from sound to ocean. The island had a three-bedroom caretaker house and an eight-bedroom clubhouse. It had steam heat with a furnace just like the one that was in Currituck School (later J.P. Knapp). When I ran it and opened it to the public, we had electricity and phone service. The way they got that out there was when VEPCO and the Carolina Phone Company wanted to run power and phone to Carova Beach—the only way the Penns would let them cross their beach property was to run power and phone to Monkey Island as well.

Back to the Twifords. Roland was born in Corolla, but he went to high school at Moyock. He stayed with his mother's brother, Mr. Luke Poole, near Currituck Courthouse during the week and went home to Monkey Island on weekends. When he grew up, he married Margaret Lindsey. They

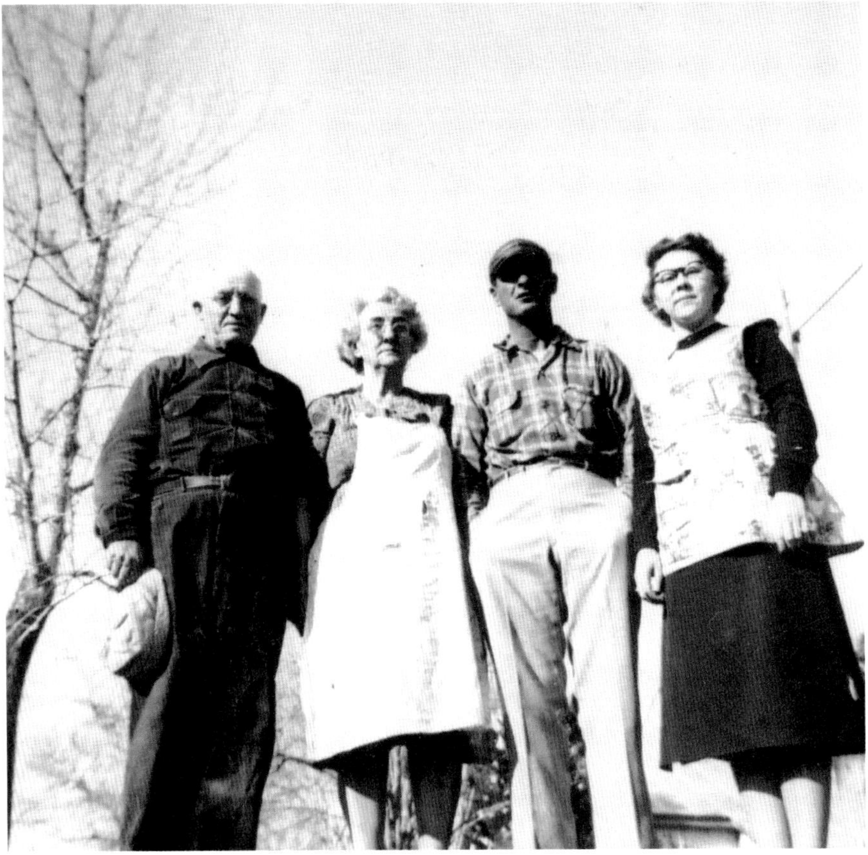

*Left to right:* Mr. George Twiford, Miss Babe Twiford, Roland Twiford and his second wife, Thelma Owens Twiford. *Courtesy of Wayne P. Twiford.*

had two children: a boy named Wayne Penn and a girl named Ailean. They divorced when Wayne was three years old. His grandmother, Miss Babe, and grandfather, Mr. George, basically raised him when he was young. His sister went to live with her grandmother Lindsey in a house on the canal bank in Coinjock. Roland later married Thelma Owens from Elizabeth City and they lived there for a while. During this time, Wayne lived with his daddy and stepmother, going to school in Elizabeth City during the week and staying at Monkey Island on weekends.

Wayne said one Christmas Day they were at Monkey Island and his daddy was going to take him hunting. He was twelve years old. He said there was a slash over there on the beach in back of Tuff Point that the snow geese had dug out. There weren't any snow geese there then, but it was full of ducks. They were tied out in the Tuff Point blind and they could

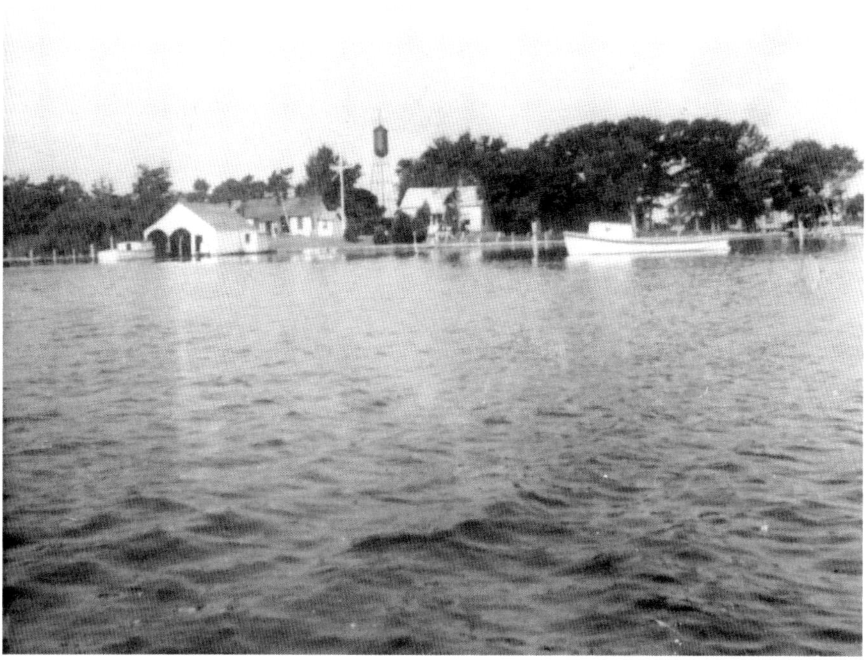

Monkey Island Club before the 1944 hurricane. *Courtesy of Wayne P. Twiford.*

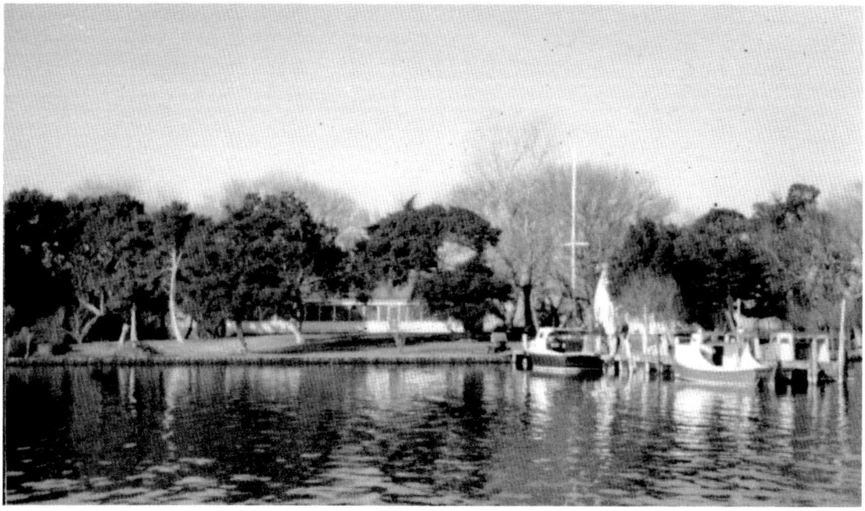

Monkey Island as it looked from 1974 to 1978, when I was running it. *Courtesy of the author.*

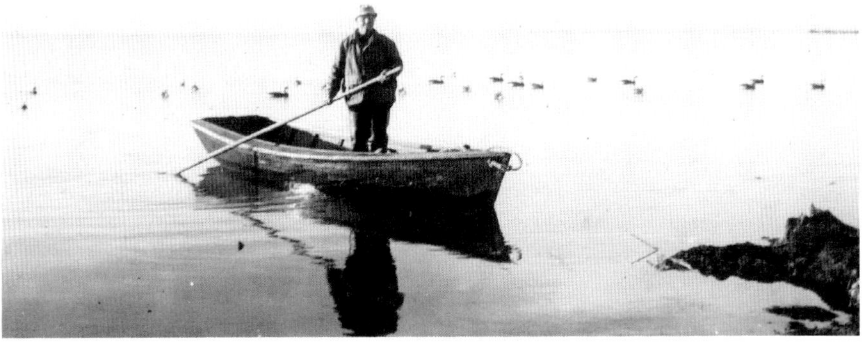

Mr. George Twiford poling out to pick up a dead goose in 1955. Note the goose in the water right beside the boat. *Courtesy of Wayne P. Twiford.*

see the ducks in that slash. Roland said, "Let's go crawl 'em." They shoved the skiff up in the marsh and tucked it in there. Roland said, "Have you some shells ready to reload, 'cause after we shoot there are going to be some singles to jump up." They crawled up to the slash and Wayne said that slash was loaded with ducks. As thick as blue peters, it looked like another one couldn't fit in there. They cut loose on them and then kept reloading. They got all the cripples they could and they picked up over forty ducks: widgeon, pintail and black ducks. The next day Wayne's granddaddy went out there with the dog and picked up twelve more.

Wayne had access to the Monkey Island property when he was growing up and that was some fantastic hunting. They had a corn room in the boathouse and they fed right much, especially when the members were coming down or, in this case, when the Penns were coming.

Wayne was looking at his daddy's log book and saw where one day he had Wayne and Joe Melson tied out in a float blind in Corney Island Channel. They killed thirty-four ruddy ducks, five redheads, one widgeon and two buffleheads.

Another day, he had Wayne and Larry Curles tied out at Ware Point on the Monkey Island Property. They got two ducks and seventeen geese. Wayne said one day he and Larry were tied out in the Parker's Bay blind and killed twenty-seven widgeon in a half day. He said his granddaddy didn't like that.

One time, Mr. Penn was coming down and they had baited up the blind on Northeast Point of Raccoon Island for him. The sound had frozen over, but by the time he got there, the sound had opened up except for some of the places around the shore. Mr. George wanted to take Mr. Ed to that blind

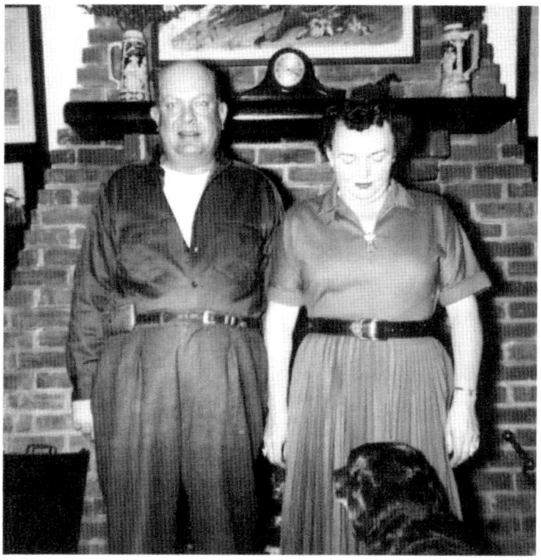

Ed Penn and his wife Bernice in front of the fireplace at Monkey Island Club. He was the oldest son of Charles A. Penn, who was one of the founders of American Tobacco Company. Charles A. Penn bought out the other members of the club in 1932, and it stayed in the Penn family until after Ed died. I sold the estate in 1974. At the time, the island was seven acres and there were three miles of beach from sound to ocean that went with it. Marcus Griggs and I spread Ed Penn's ashes on Monkey Island and Currituck Sound. *Courtesy of Wayne P. Twiford.*

they had baited and try those canvasbacks, but Mr. Ed wanted to go to the east side of Mary Island, so that's where they went.

Wayne said it was a slick calm day and he was by himself so he went to Southeast Island. He didn't do much. Killed a duck or two. He took up and was heading to Monkey Island in a fifteen-foot skiff with a five-horsepower outboard on her. When he got around the point of Raccoon Island, he began to notice those canvasbacks. They were falling out and going to Northeast Point. Wayne said to himself, "I'm going over there and just tie me out some canvasback decoys." He had about a dozen canvasback decoys in the boat. Said it was just him and the dog. "I'd never seen anything like it in my life," he said. "The canvasback would go in there and light in the decoys. They'd keep going in when I was shooting! I killed twenty-seven." Wayne said it was odd that it was the same number from another trip, but that was the way it was.

"Since it was slick calm, everybody all over the sound could hear me shoot and I got a little bit worried. I gathered the ducks up and put four on a string. That was the limit." Wayne said he put the rest of them in the marsh under a muskrat bed. He was going to go back that night to get them. He was taking up decoys and there were cripples all over the place. He said he heard this outboard motor and looked up and a boat was coming flying. "Good God, there's the game warden." He had a twenty-five-horsepower Johnson outboard, one of the first big outboard motors that Wayne had ever seen around here. While Wayne was watching, Albert Sumrell hit a stump and broke the sheer pin on the motor and had to take the motor off the stern of the boat and lay it down in the boat to fix it. Wayne said he was watching him and his adrenaline was pumping.

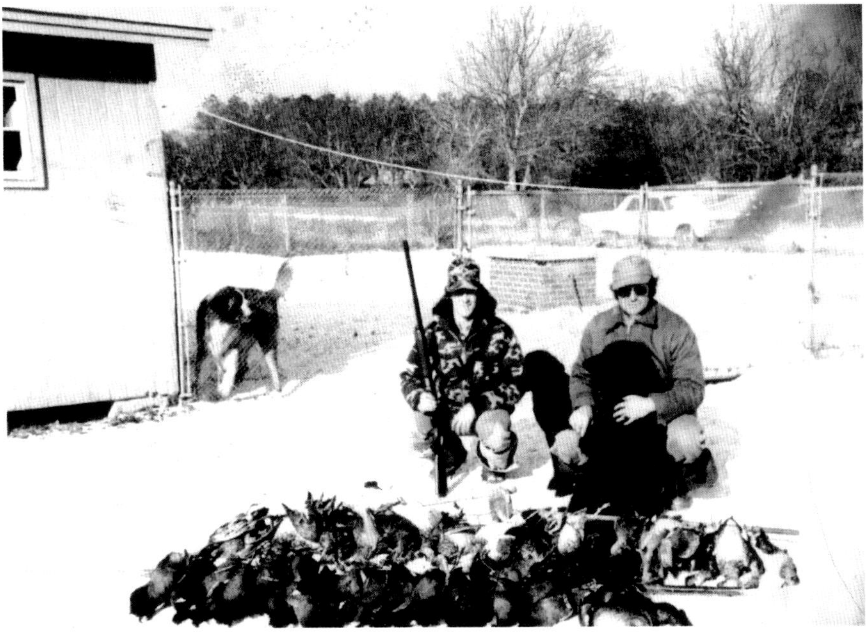

January 13, 1982, at Piney Island Bay: thirty-eight ducks, thirty-two blue peters and five geese. At that time, their limit was probably four or five ducks each, fifteen blue peters and one or two geese. I know to kill that much game in Piney Island Bay in 1982, they were either shooting over corn or shooting in an ice hole. They have cleaned up their act now and don't do that kind of violating. *Courtesy of Wayne P. Twiford.*

He finished taking up decoys and went back to the blind to get his gear and his dog, then started back to Monkey Island. He had just gone about two hundred yards when Albert got his motor fixed and came by him within fifty feet, but didn't stop him. He said he guessed he figured it was too late then. When he got to Monkey Island, Wayne found out he had messed up. He had four ducks in the bow and four ducks in the stern. If Albert had stopped him, he would'a had him.

Wayne said that night he and his daddy went back to get the ducks. He thought he could go right to them, but they tore up half the muskrat beds in that marsh before they found them. His daddy was very upset with him. His granddaddy was upset with him, too, because Ed Penn had just killed one black duck! He told Wayne, "Now, here's what I want you to do. Take some of those canvasback and give them to Ed and tell him to give some of them to his mama. You've messed up here, Wayne. You've rubbed this man the wrong way."

Wayne said his daddy, Roland and Mr. Willard Fulcher used to do a little firelighting. He said they had it down pat. They knew what to do. It was very effective. People started complaining about it, they were getting so brazen about it.

The game wardens put together kind of a SWAT team. Roland and Mr. Fulcher came in and hid their game down on the point south of the house. Although it was at night, the game wardens saw where they put their game (including a swan this time) and they went and got it. Wayne said his daddy had to go to court and pay $250. Back then, that was about a month's wages. They gave the swan to the school and they served it for lunch one day. He said lunch was twenty cents. When Wayne went through the line, he told the lady he didn't think he ought to have to pay since his daddy had already paid $250 for that swan. The following is an excerpt from the *Daily Advance*, dated Thursday, January 17, 1952, courtesy of June Sumrell Pell:

> *Large Haul is Made by Game Protectors in Currituck County*
>
> *State game protectors in Currituck County Wednesday night caught two hunters who were firelighting for geese, ducks and swan and seized six swan, 12 geese, and 15 coot or Blue Peters.*
>
> *Permanent Protector R. A. Dowdy who led the raid on the hunters, said that the two men in a skiff were firelighting at Churches Island in Currituck County in the marshes. He declined to release the names of the two men, saying that they will be arrested later by a U.S. Marshall on charges of hunting out of season, firelighting, shooting swan and maybe other counts.*
>
> *The hunters who were presumed to have a market for the wildfowl, were using a modern firelighting lantern. It was driven by a storage battery on the boat. They fired only nine shots to get the entire batch of more than 200 pounds of wildfowl meat, the arresting officer said.*
>
> *Participating in the raid on the firelighters in addition to Dowdy were Special Officers Howard Forbes, Howard Sumrell, and Milburn Sawyer.*
>
> *They said the men apparently did all their shooting just before 9 o'clock Wednesday night and then brought in the kill around 11 o'clock. The officers were standing nearby waiting for the men when they threw the wildfowl out of the boat.*
>
> *District Supervisor Leon K. Thomas of Edenton said that intense efforts have been underway in Currituck County to catch firelighters since the wildfowl season closed on January 5. He said officers have spent several nights along the waterfront looking for the violators. The two men probably will stand trial in Elizabeth City in February or March. Heavy fines and penalties are imposed for shooting out of season and especially for shooting Swan.*
>
> *Names of the two men who did the killing will be released, the officer said, as soon as they are officially arrested.*

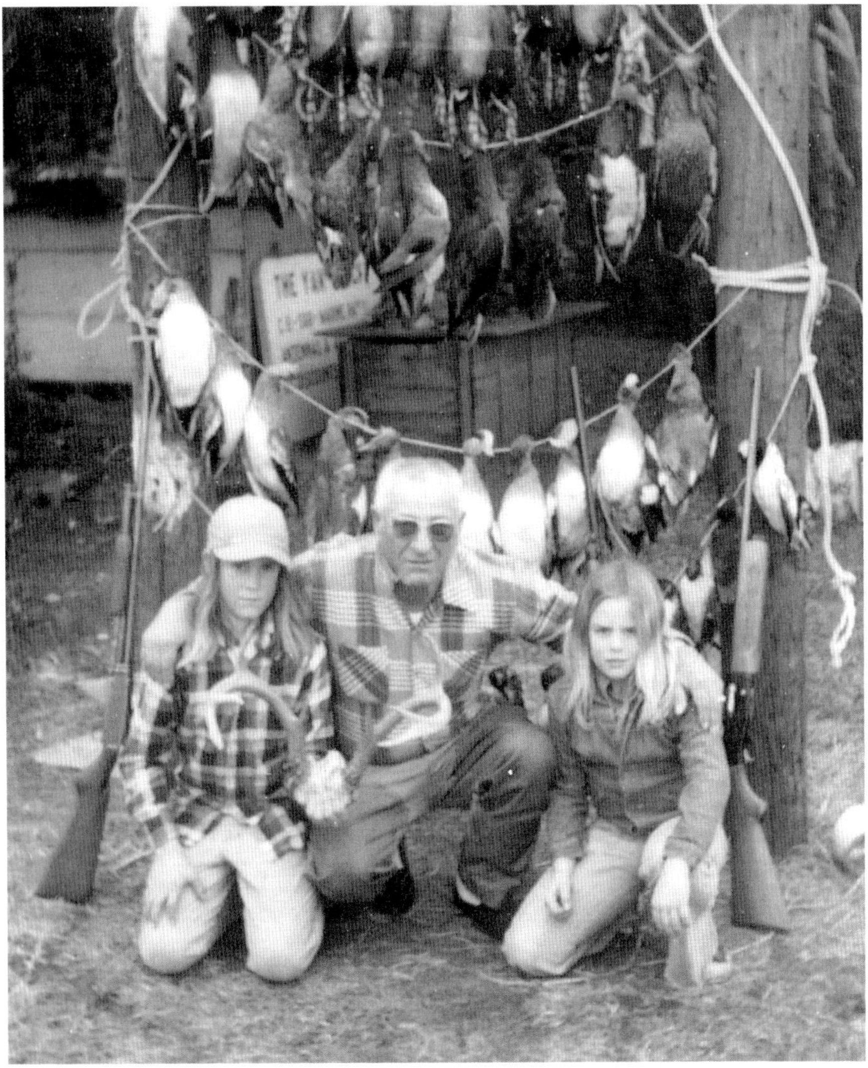

Roland Twiford and his two grandsons, Wayne Jr. (left) and Darrell. They look like girls in this picture, but they're all boy. *Courtesy of Wayne P. Twiford.*

Larry Woodhouse told me that Mr. Emerson Sears, who lived on Churches Island and owned land that went back to Old Field Creek, kept calling Larry's daddy, Orville, and telling him somebody was firelighting geese and swans in Old Field Creek every Saturday night. One night Miss Ola said, "Orville, send somebody up there before that man drives us crazy." He called Scott Sawyer, one of the game wardens, and told him to check it out. Scott did this, and who did he catch but Mr. Em! Scott called

Mr. Orville and asked him what he wanted him to do. I don't know what his answer was, but Mr. Em soon called Orville raising Cain because he had sent the game warden on the wrong night! I can remember Mr. Em always being in the store and saying, "I gosh, there was somebody back there in Old Field Creek firelighting those geese and swan last night." Everybody knew it was him.

Wayne and I were talking about how Charlie Snowden used to buy game. He told me one time Charlie said to Wayne's daddy, "Roland, I want some blue peters." Roland asked, "How many do you want, Charlie?" Charlie said, "I want all you can get." There used to be a lot of eagles here and Wayne said there was always a raft of blue peters around Monkey Island. One afternoon, he and his daddy were sitting there in a skiff in the boathouse at Monkey Island with their guns ready, waiting for an eagle to come get after the blue peters, which would cause them to bunch up. Just before dark, here came two eagles, working on those blue peters. They didn't have an outboard motor then. Wayne had a double-barrel shotgun and his daddy had a five-shot Browning automatic. He said they shoved up there just right. Those blue peters were so close together they were just about standing on one another. They shot seven times and picked up 360 blue peters. They put them in burlap sacks and went across the sound and went up to Charlie Snowden's house in Maple. They had the whole trunk of the car full of sacks of blue peters. He went up to the house, found Charlie and said, "Charlie, I got you some blue peters." Charlie said, "Okay." Roland asked him to go out and help them get them. When he opened the trunk, Charlie said, "Good Lord, Roland, how many did you get?"

"Three hundred and sixty."

"Well, I told you to get all you could, so I'll pay you for them."

Wayne told me Charlie Snowden had asked him for some swans one time and he'd gotten him six. He said several months later, he was on a tugboat going up the James River to Richmond. Before he left that morning, he picked up a *Virginian-Pilot*. When he got around to reading it, he saw where Charlie Snowden had been charged with possession of a swan. Of course, he knew where that swan came from. He could hardly wait to get to a telephone so he could call somebody and find out what was going on. When he finally got to a phone, he found out. Charlie and Gene Poyner were running the Bayview Service Station at the intersection of U.S. 158 and U.S. 168 at Barco, when a man had gone in posing as a salesman of chocolate-covered peanuts. He set everybody up with beer and seemed to be a real nice guy. He told Charlie he'd like to find out where he could buy some swans and geese. He said he and his family loved that stuff and said he didn't need a whole lot, just one or two. Charlie said to himself, "I'm

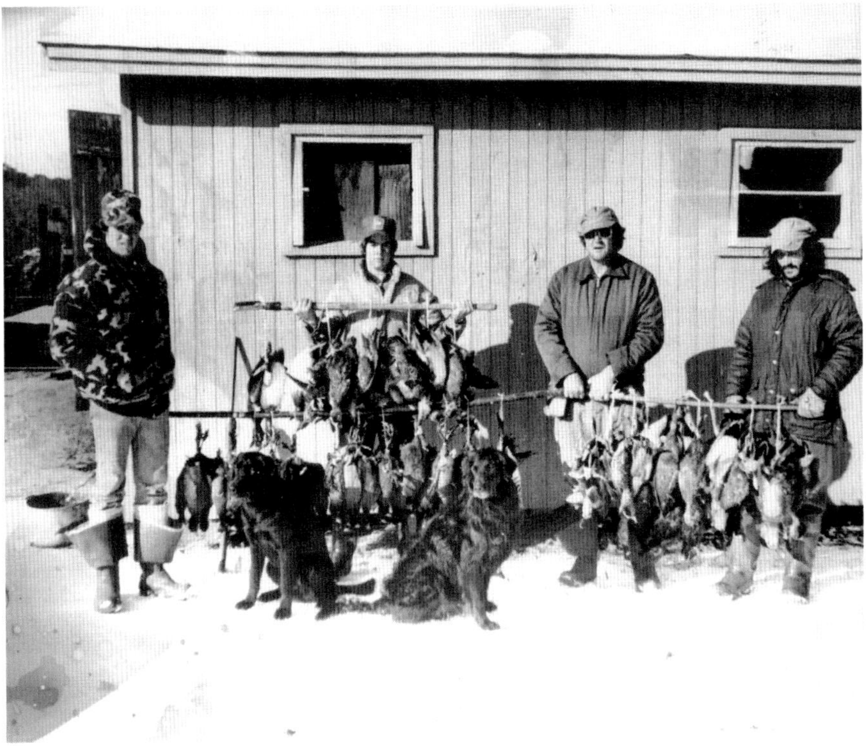

*Left to right:* Wayne Jr., Darrell, Wayne Penn Twiford and Wayne's son-in-law Allen Speight. *Courtesy of Wayne P. Twiford.*

not going to sell him anything, but I do have that one swan at home in the freezer." Charlie said, "I'll give you a goose"—he wasn't about to tell him it was a swan—and he sent someone up to the house with the guy to get the bird. Wayne said the man knew it was a swan and he busted Charlie. He got Bud Lupton, too. Come to find out, it was a "sting" he was doing up and down the coast. He said that cleaned up his act right then. Besides being illegal, it was getting so that kind of thing was no longer socially acceptable as it once had been.

I remember one time when I was a little boy, if my granddaddy Wib Boswood and grandmother Carrie Boswood wanted a goose, he would go back to the landing at night. I'd hear him shoot a time or two and he'd come back with a goose. He died May 14, 1941, so that's been a long time ago.

Wayne used to crawl geese up and down the shore at Waterlily because geese would come ashore at night, whereas swans would come ashore in the daytime and go offshore at night.

Wayne said his daddy was a really good duck hunter. He was out in the sound every day and knew where the best place to go was, depending on the way the wind was blowing. He guided for Casey Jones most of the time. He and Woodrow Whitson were good friends and he guided for Woodrow some, but mostly Casey. Wayne said that he guided for Woodrow a couple of years, too.

"When I was growing up," Wayne said, "you didn't kill ducks every day, but there'd be some days when you'd kill sixty ducks. I've done that a few times."

We got to talking about good places to tie out a float rig. I told him one of my favorite ties was on the Gull Rock if I could beat Mr. Ligee (Elijah) Tate there. It used to be about three acres and was shaped like a horseshoe with the opening facing south. It had about two and a half or three feet of water on it with a normal tide. It was right in the middle of the sound, maybe a little closer to the west side. If you left Casey Jones's dock and headed right for Currituck Beach (Corolla) Light, you would run right across the top of it. I've laid in bed many a night when I had sportsmen the next day and heard that wind howling, knowing if I could beat Mr. Ligee and Mr. Frank Carter to the Gull Rock, I could lay there in most any kind of wind. It would be calmer on the Gull Rock and that would make your decoys show up better too. On a rough day, I've seen Mr. Ligee tie an oily rag around the neck of the last decoy in the string. The oil slick would get the attention of the ducks and they would see his decoys. Just two nights ago—January 2, 2008—I was lying in bed listening to that wind howl and reminiscing about those days I just talked about. The difference is I didn't have sportsmen the next day, but I'd promised to go hunting in my float rig with my grandson, Chet Morris, and his friend, Alex Evans. The temperature was supposed to be about twenty degrees and the wind blowing twenty-five or thirty miles per hour from the northwest. I went and made out pretty good for a seventy-five-year-old man. I guess it's just in my blood.

Mr. Frank Carter had two float-blind rigs and Wayne said he ran one of them for Mr. Frank for two years. The first time he guided for him, Mr. Frank called him up the night before and said, "Wayne, I think you need to go to the southeast corner of the Gull Rock tomorrow. I'll tell you why. I think we got a shift coming." We didn't get a lot of weather reports back then like we do now. You'd read the signs and watch the barometer. Wayne said Mr. Frank was an expert at that. He said the wind is going to shift and blow northwest for a while. It may die down a little after the shift. Wayne said Mr. Frank was right. The next morning, you could see that bank in the northwest and it beared down and blew, but he was okay on the Gull Rock.

As I told Wayne, Mr. Casey Jones told me that when you see a bank of clouds in the east of a morning, the higher the bank is, the harder it's going to blow. I've found that to be true. A lot of mornings I'd come down to the dock and he'd say, "Boy, you better put her behind a shoal today." I've tried to teach my grandsons that, but I'm not sure they think I know anything.

That's kinda' like when I got my first gas boat at age fifteen. I talked Mama and Daddy into letting me take all my savings, $350, that I'd made driving a tractor for Uncle Tommy when he was farming and from mowing grass for people. I bought an old gas boat from Vernon Lee Creekmore.

When I got that boat, Mr. Earl Snowden took me and showed me where to look out for logs, stumps and sunken pilings all around Coinjock Bay and the north part of the sound. Most of that stuff is still there under the water. I've tried to teach it to my grandsons. I don't know if they listen or not. It scares me when I see people skiing over old piers and the like because I know what's down there.

# Night the Boat Broke Down

Wayne was about ten years old and he was living in Elizabeth City with his daddy and stepmother. On Friday afternoon, he'd catch the Trailways bus from Elizabeth City to Coinjock. His granddaddy would meet him and they would go to Waterlily, get in the boat and go to Monkey Island. On Sunday afternoon, they'd reverse the process.

On this particular afternoon, even though it was in the winter, it was not very cold and Wayne didn't have heavy clothes on. Before they got to Monkey Island, the engine ran hot. Mr. George ran her real slow and tried to nurse her along and make it to the island, but she got so hot she cut off and froze up. They later found out the strainer under the bottom of the water intake had come off and the intake had stopped up with grass.

It was getting on toward dark and it was getting rough. There was a dark-looking cloud in the northwest. His granddaddy had an anchor in the stern of the boat. It was blowing so hard then that Mr. George was afraid to try to get up to the bow to tie the anchor on up there so he just tied it to the stern cleat and threw it overboard. The wind came northwest and blew a gale and turned freezing cold. She was a big old boat, at least thirty feet long with a big cabin, but she had no heater. Wayne didn't have on thick clothes and he was cold.

The boat started dragging anchor and took up on a shoal. He didn't know where, but he thought it was southeast of Mary Island. His granddaddy told him they had to stay awake—if they went to sleep they'd freeze to death.

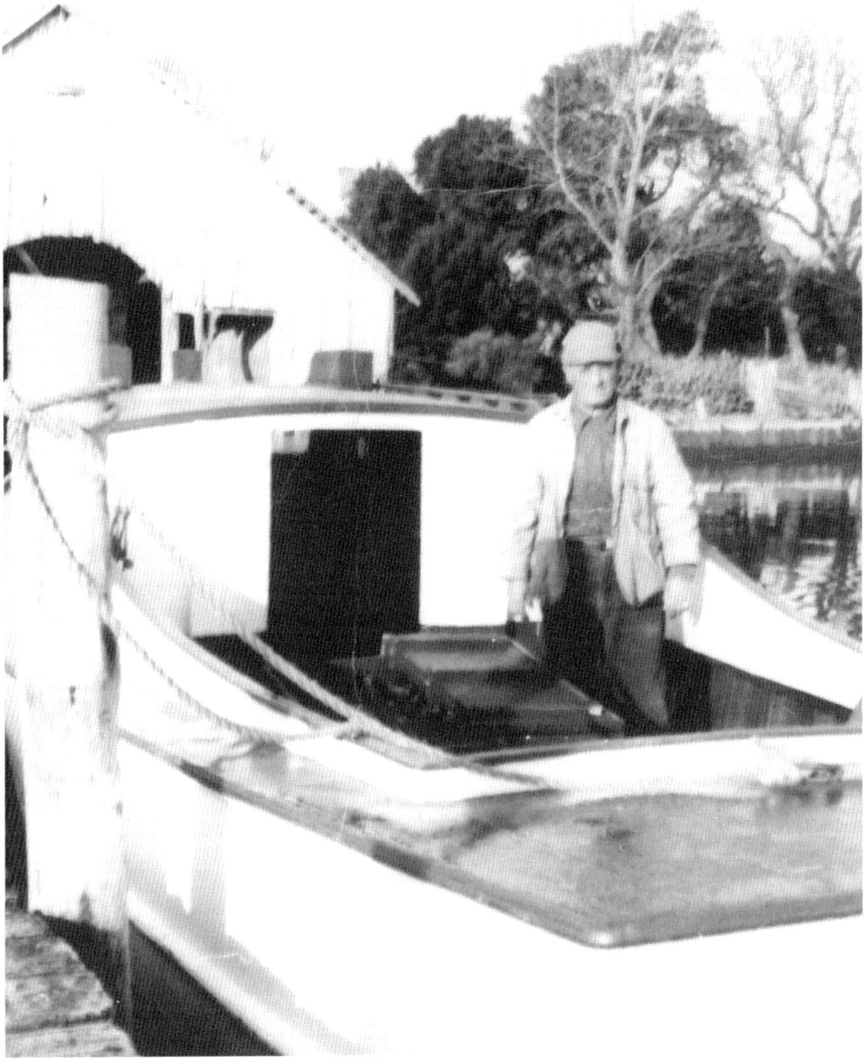

George Twiford in the Monkey Island boat in which he and his grandson, Wayne Penn Twiford, spent the night in Currituck Sound. *Courtesy of Wayne P. Twiford.*

He'd start to doze off and his granddaddy would tell him to bark like Stokes, a big old Chesapeake retriever they had. Seas were breaking over the stern and the water was running forward. Nobody had electric bilge pumps then, just galvanized hand pumps. Mr. George took a floor board up in the cabin and he had a five-gallon bucket he'd pump full, then he'd open the cabin door and dump it overboard. Wayne said he hated to see that door open and let that cold air in.

Every drop that was flying was freezing. Mr. George would go out every now and then with a hammer and beat the ice off to keep the boat from getting too heavy.

Mr. Pell Austin was in the Coast Guard, stationed at Corolla, and they had a boat there. He said about daybreak, Mr. Pell and two or three other men came and got them and took them to Monkey Island. He said when they got there, his grandmother (Miss Babe) was standing on the dock wringing her hands and crying. I know she was worried to death because at that time there was no communication to the island. In fact, I don't know how anybody knew they were missing. Wayne didn't know either, but word got out somehow because Mr. Frank Carter and Roland (Wayne's daddy) looked all night for them in Mr. Frank's boat. She had a cabin but no windshield, and he said their foul-weather gear was nothing but a solid sheet of ice. They had been looking for them all night. They went to Poplar Branch and got Mr. Norman Gregory to get them some more gas.

A happy ending to what could have been a sad story. I remember this, as it was the topic of conversation in Coinjock. It took place sometime in the 1940s.

# Ralph Barco

Ralph Barco farmed, had a roadside produce market, carried sportsmen and did whatever he could to make a living in Currituck, like a lot of other natives. He married Norma Saunders (her daddy, Elle and two of her brothers, Ralph and Blanton, are mentioned elsewhere in this book).

They built the hunting lodge in 1958. It is now the clubhouse for Goose Creek Golf Course. Ralph was kinda' like Woodrow Whitson in that he could keep the sportsmen entertained spinning yarns whether they killed any ducks or not. His son Randy told me that the people who guided there were Ralph, his brother Wendell, William Earl Wright, the Guard boys (John, James, Jack and Jeff), Sid Wright, Barry Walker and Randy, when he got old enough.

Norma looked after the kitchen with the help of a colored woman named Pearl and her sister Bertie Erickson. Mary Corbell made the lunches and took care of the housecleaning.

Ralph had mostly open-water blinds and some marsh blinds. He had his own private dock. You went through a cornfield to get to his dock on Currituck Sound. Randy said every few years his daddy and his Uncle Wendell would dynamite the channel when it would fill up.

Ralph's lodge was not like the club hunting, which were mostly ponds and marsh blinds. It was like Woodrow Whitson's, Colon and Dorothy Grandy's, G.C. Sawyer's and others. Sportsmen would pay to come duck

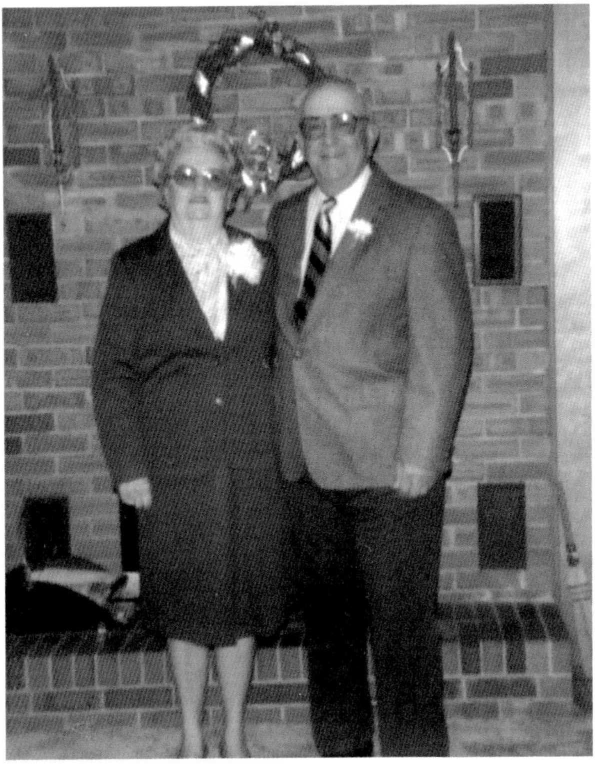

Norma and Ralph Barco in front of the fireplace in their hunting lodge. *Courtesy of Randy Barco.*

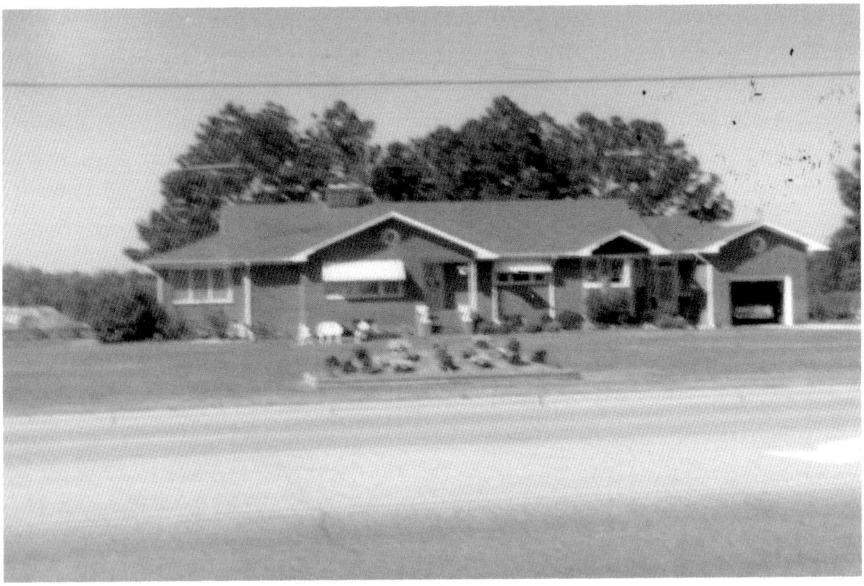

Ralph Barco's hunting lodge, built in 1958. It is now the clubhouse for Goose Creek Golf Course. *Courtesy of Randy Barco.*

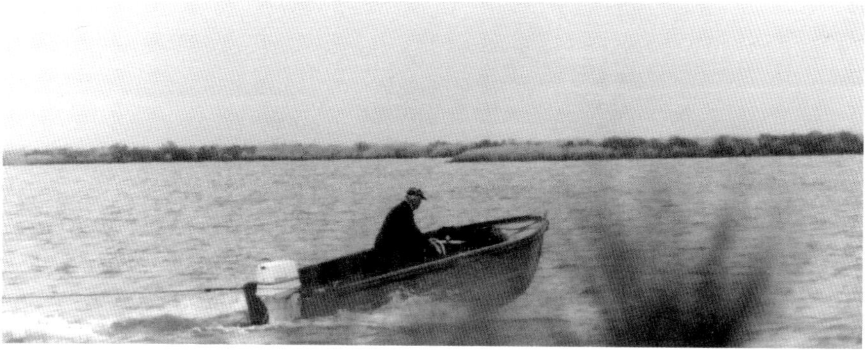

Ralph Barco towing a skiff going to a duck blind in Currituck Sound. *Courtesy of Randy Barco.*

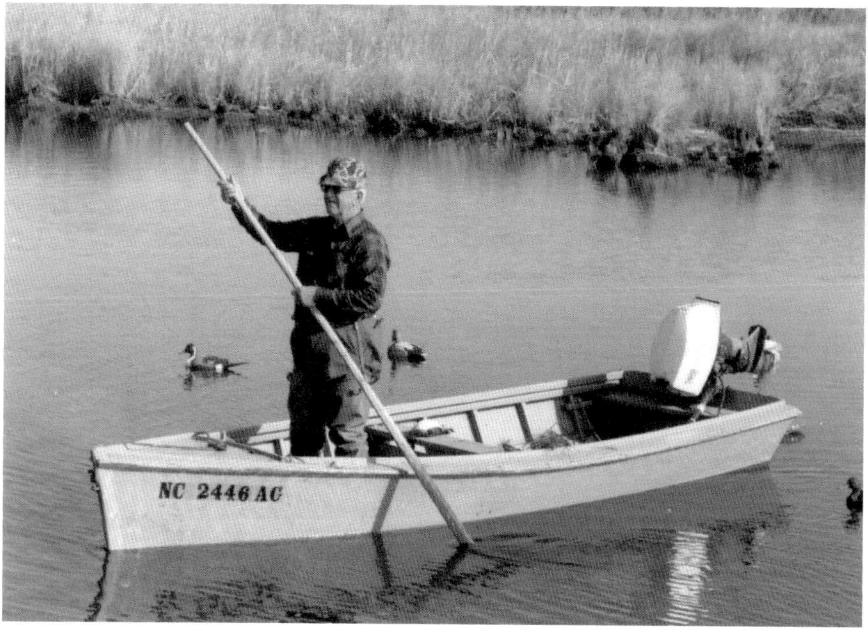


Ralph Barco has been out to pick up a dead duck. Note the duck on the seat of the skiff. *Courtesy of Randy Barco.*

hunting. They would get room and board and a guide. They didn't come in for lunch. They packed a lunch and stayed out all day.

There was a cornfield between the road and the dock that Randy said geese would go in everyday. He said they'd kill their limit of geese by 9:00 a.m. in the cornfield and then go in the sound and get their ducks. How times have changed.

# Game Wardens

I talked with Mike Pell about his granddaddy, Howard Sumrell. Mr. Howard was a county game warden hired by the Currituck County Game Commission. Later, these game wardens were appointed by the state and called "special game wardens." Mr. Howard's brother, Albert, was a federal game warden. I spoke of him in the story about Charlie Dozier and G.C. Sawyer.

Mike's mother, June Pell, said when Mike was a little boy he used to go to Norfolk market to sell tomatoes with Mr. Howard (her daddy). Her daddy would tell Mike stories about when he was game warden. The following are some of the stories Mike told me.

Mr. Howard was on a patrol one day up around Knotts Island Bay. He heard all this shooting up at the north end of the island, so he decided he'd go up there and check it out. When he got there, he found it to be a long blind and the boys had all gone to the other end of the blind with a big pile of game. The boys had built the blind right across the North Carolina–Virginia line. The marker was right nearby, so you could see the blind was in both states. They got real nasty and mouthy and said, "You can't do nothin' to us! We're in Virginia!" He said, "Well, I guess you boys got me," so he left.

The next day, he went and got his brother Albert and went back up there. They were shooting and killing ducks just like they had been the day before. The ducks had to have been baited to go in there like that. When

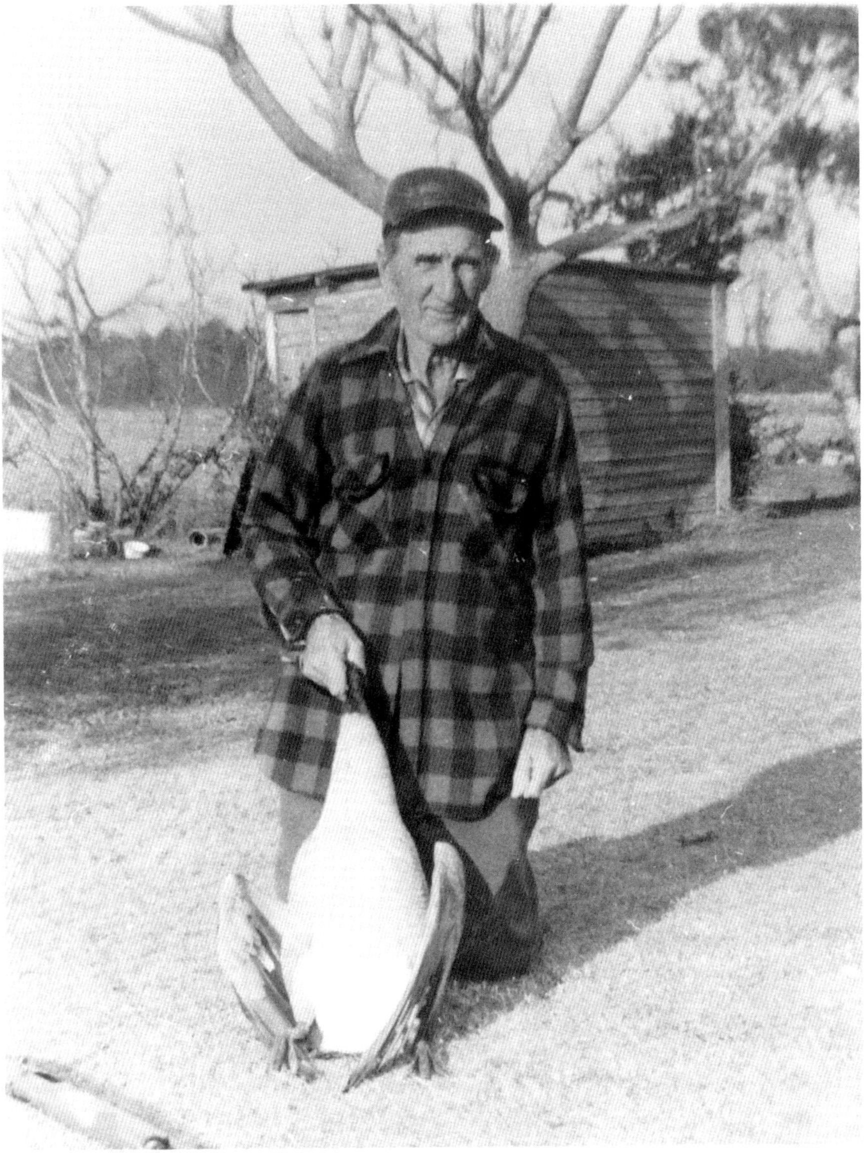

Special Game Warden Howard Sumrell. *Courtesy of June Pell.*

they went up to them, the boys said, "We told you yesterday you can't touch us 'cause we're in Virginia." Mr. Howard said, "Fellows, I want to introduce you to my brother, Albert Sumrell. He's a federal game warden and he can take care of you no matter which end of the blind you're in." They really looked surprised. Mr. Albert wrote them all tickets to go to federal court.

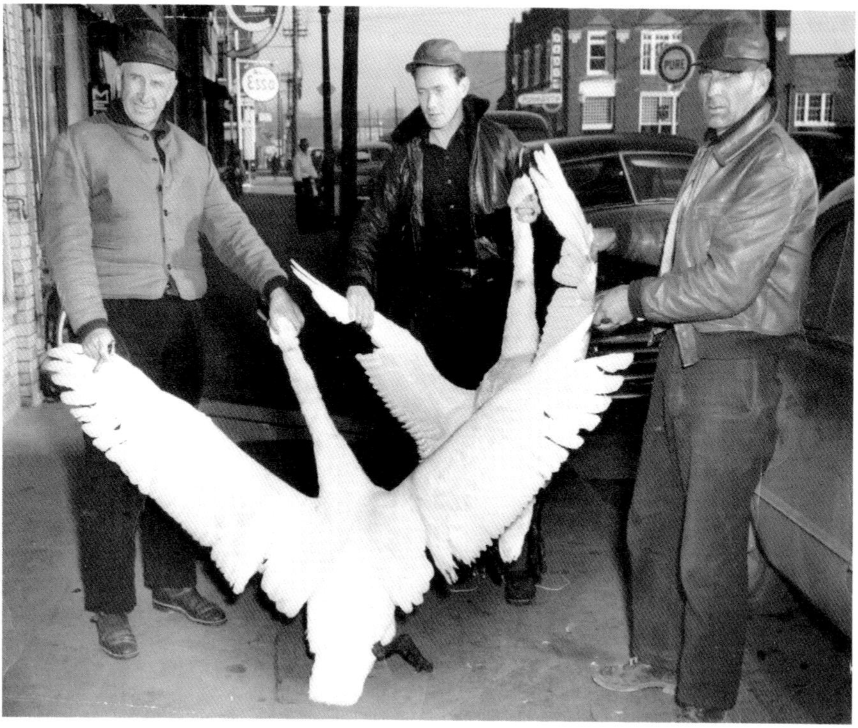


*Left to right:* Federal Game Wardens Albert Sumrell and Robert Halstead, and Special Game Warden Howard Sumrell. *Courtesy of June Pell.*

Another story Mike told me was about the time his granddaddy and two more wardens were going to catch some firelighters one night. They left Poplar Branch Landing and it wasn't long before it set in to snowing so hard you couldn't see. They kept running around trying to get back to Poplar Branch; they couldn't see and were lost. Finally, they ran out of gas. They poled up on some marsh, pulled the boat up on the marsh and turned it up on its side for a windbreak. They got so cold they thought they were going to freeze to death. They even tried to set the boat afire, but couldn't get it to light.

When it finally got light, they could see they were on the marsh right close to Currituck Club, so they walked up there. The club men took them in by the fire and there was a doctor there. He kept taking their pulse and temperature and kept giving them teaspoons of whiskey until they got warmed up. He said they really thought they were going to freeze to death.

Maybe I should tell about my experience with Albert Sumrell. One day, I had my float box tied out in Coinjock Bay about one thousand yards southwest of the north point of Long Point Island. I had Jerry Hardesty and Gordon Sawyer in the float box. Jerry was the Currituck County

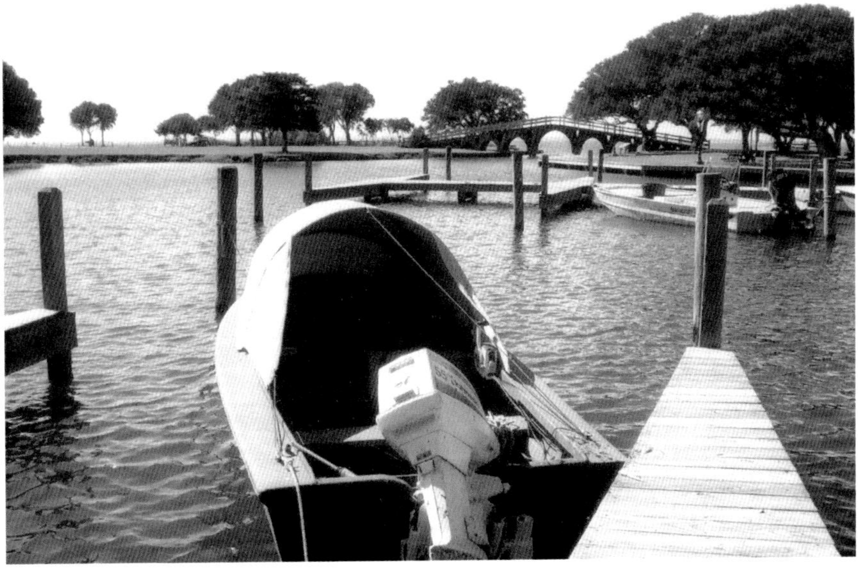

Blanton Saunders built this boat for the North Carolina Wildlife Commission in 1972 for Warden Howard Forbes Jr. to run. Howard Jr. told me Blanton charged the state $350 to build the boat and spray hood. The state supplied the motor and controls. Howard Jr. told me he gave a man a ticket for fishing without a license one time and the man said, "If you'd have been in a boat that looked like a game warden's, you'd never have caught me." When Howard Jr. retired, the state gave him the boat. He gave her to the Whalehead Preservation Trust and Jimmy Markert restored her in 2006. This picture was taken at the Whalehead Club in 2007. *Courtesy of the author.*

agricultural agent and Gordon was the assistant. My wife, Frances, was their secretary. They were both close friends of ours. I was waiting on them with my gas boat, *Rhonda.*

The boys had a cripple down and I was riding around in circles looking for him. I finally gave up and rode down the bay a ways to see if I saw any ducks. I had paying sportsmen the next day and I wanted to see where I should tie out. I came back to my stake blind and tied *Rhonda* there while I sat there and ate a sandwich. I knew Albert Sumrell was sitting down on the south end of Long Point. I saw him sitting there up against the marsh in his outboard motorboat. Now, you know I wasn't going to violate any laws that I knew of with him looking at me.

About the time I finished eating my sandwich, I heard the boys shoot. I untied *Rhonda* and was heading to the float box as quick as I could in case they had another cripple—maybe I could get him before he got away. Another thing was that the old boat leaked and we didn't have automatic bilge pumps back then, just hand pumps. Plus, *Rhonda* had a plug in the bottom in the stern with a scoop under it so it would drain all the water out as long as you were going fast. When you slowed up, you had to put the plug in or the water would come back in. I had the plug out to bail her out. I was looking ahead where I was going. When I looked back to put the plug in, I saw Albert Sumrell right beside me motioning for me to stop. I had to put the plug in before I could stop. I did this as quickly as possible and stopped. He wanted to know why I didn't stop. I told him I didn't see him until I turned to put the plug in and I had to do that before I could stop.

"You were carousing the boobies [local name for ruddy ducks]," he said.

"I was looking for a cripple duck," I said. Next he looked over into the boat and said, "There's a grain of corn." "Yea, it sure is," I said, and picked it up and threw it overboard.

"Well, you may hear from this again or you may not." He went on and I went back to waiting on my float box. In a few days, I got a summons to go before Judge Larkin at Elizabeth City Federal Court. Now I found out what the problem was. My Daddy, Judge Chester Morris, had been friends with Albert Sumrell for many years, but they had just gotten cross-legged about something—something political. Now I could see he was after me to get at Daddy. I guess that's the way the world goes.

Long story short, Daddy hired Gerald White as my attorney and I went to federal court. Among other notables whose names I don't remember, I had United States Deputy Marshal Will Flora as a character witness. I was sitting up there in the prisoner's dock with all the bootleggers and others on trial for federal offenses. Gerald White passed me a note telling me how much time the judge could give me.

When my case came up, the judge asked Mr. Sumrell what the charges were. He said carousing game and running from a game warden. When I got on the stand, I had a Coast and Geodetic Survey chart of Coinjock Bay. I had drawn exactly where I had been on the chart and showed it to the judge. I told him why I was looking around—because I had sportsmen the next day. As to running from Mr. Sumrell, I said, "Your Honor, I'm not dumb enough to think this old gas boat will outrun Mr. Sumrell's fast outboard motorboat." When I told the judge about going over to the blind and tying up to eat a sandwich at 7:00 a.m., he asked, "You start eating your lunch at 7:00 a.m.?" I said, "Your Honor, I take about ten sandwiches with me, and anytime after daybreak I'm subject to start eating." The courtroom went in an uproar. When Mr. Sumrell was talking about me coursing, the judge asked him if I knew what I was doing. Mr. Sumrell said, "Oh, yeah, he knew what he was doing all right."

The judge dismissed the case and said the reason he did was because of the chart I'd shown him showing what I did. I was really innocent in this

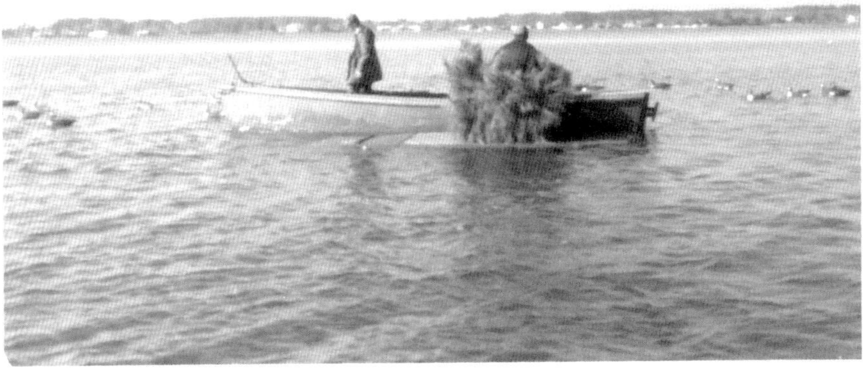

This picture is of the float box that I was using the day Albert Sumrell gave me the ticket. My son, Walton Morris, is in my old twenty-three-foot decoy skiff built by Pat O'Neal in 1947. As of this writing, I still own her and the float box and they are both useable. The problem is that Walt's quit hunting and my grandsons say it's too much trouble to tie out all that rig when there are not many ducks. *Courtesy of the author.*

case. I will admit I've swum many a goose, and if I do say so myself, I was pretty good at it. When I had sportsmen, they may not kill many ducks, but I could usually get a bunch of geese to them.

# Wallace O'Neal

Much of the information that I have on Wallace O'Neal Sr. comes from *A Heritage of Currituck County,* which was edited by Jo Anna Heath Bates (1985). Wallace O'Neal Sr. lived in Duck, North Carolina, on a float house that was tied up to a landing dock there. He made his living fishing. While there, he met his future wife, Rosanna Harris. They lived first at Corolla, then moved to Waterlily and lived at what is now the Nesbitt property, a home named Currituck Cedar Farm. He later moved to Aydlett, where he farmed, took sportsmen in at his Wild Game Inn and commercial fished. During hunting season, Rosanna managed the lodge (cooking for the hunters and so forth) while he guided hunters. He and Rosanna had ten children, all of whom learned to help keep the family farm going. Between them, they helped their parents with the plowing, sewing, cooking, livestock tending, cleaning and other chores. Both Wallace and Wallace Jr. made a lot of working decoys. In 1946, he sold the farm to Mark Doxey but kept his Wild Game Inn and his house.

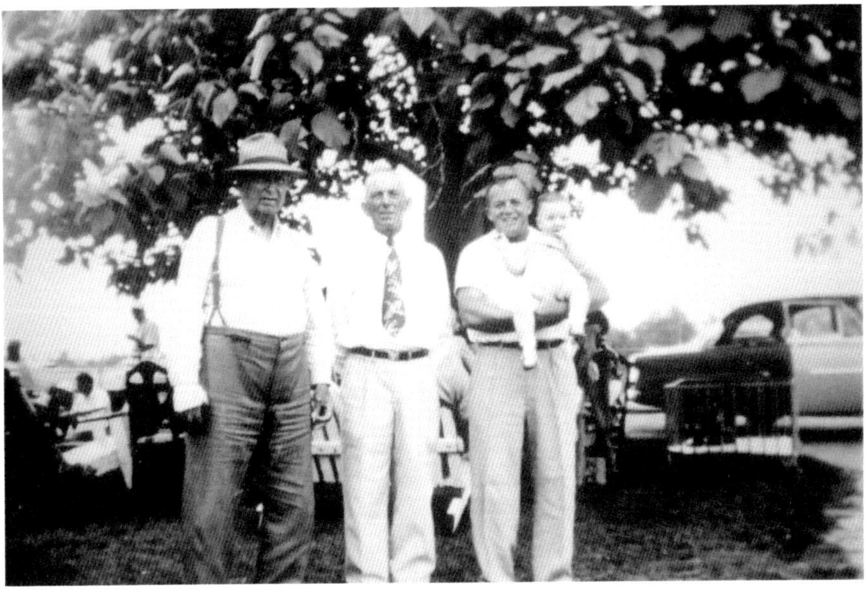

Wallace O'Neal Sr., Wallace Jr. and Wallace III holding Wallace IV. *Courtesy of Mike Doxey.*

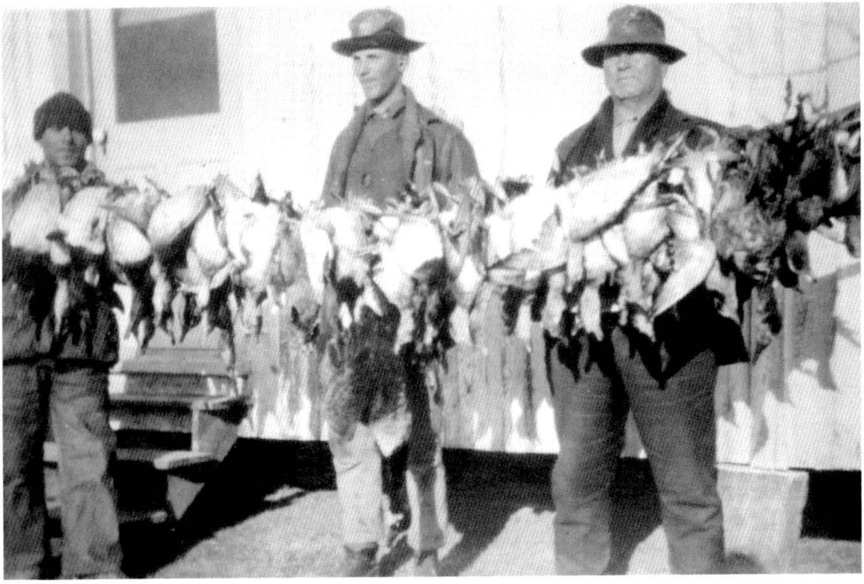

Dewey O'Neal, Alonzo Saunders and Wallace O'Neal Sr. standing in front of the Wild Game Inn. *Courtesy of Mike Doxey.*

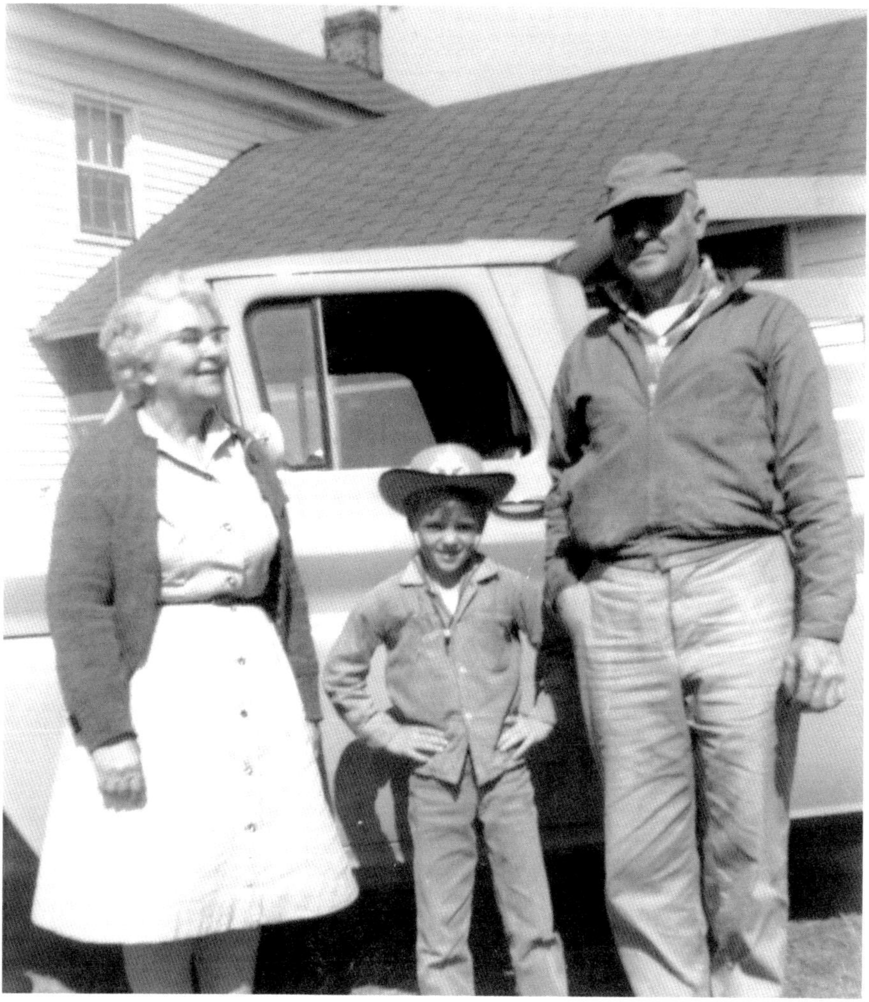

Edna Doxey, grandson Mike Doxey and Mark Doxey. The farm, as of this writing, is still in Mark Doxey's family. *Courtesy of Mike Doxey.*

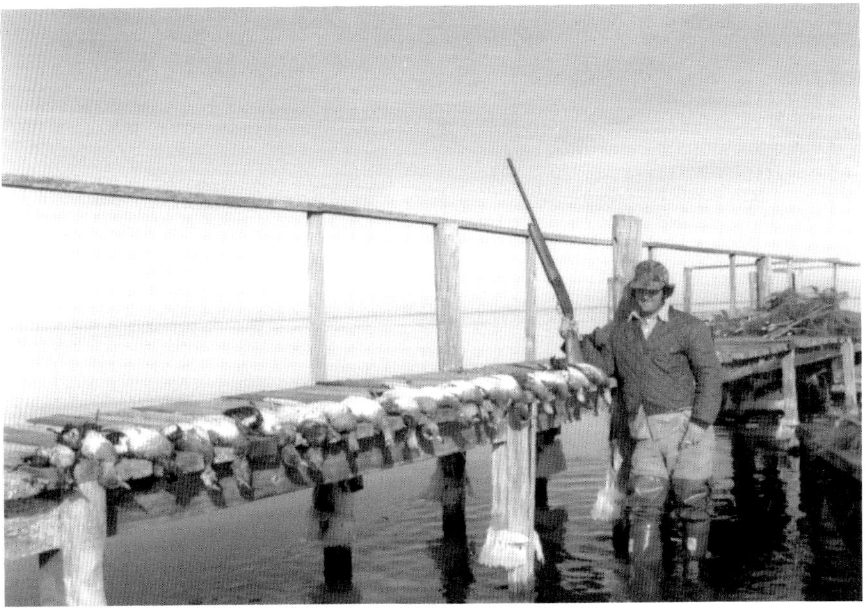

Mike Doxey with a good day's hunt in 1977. Mike's mother, Clarine Doxey, cooked for many years at Pine Island Club for Mr. Earl Slick. After Clarine retired, her daughter, Patricia Doxey Leary, took over her mother's job and is still cooking at Pine Island as of this writing. *Courtesy of Mike Doxey.*

# Currituck Time

Jerry Wright was in my office today, April 24, 2008, and told me two stories that I thought too good not to include in this book.

Jerry was appointed to the North Carolina Wildlife Commission in 1981. He said the first thing he did was go see Mr. Orville Woodhouse since Mr. Orville had been on the commission for twenty-six years. Mr. Orville told Jerry that the biggest problem he would have was with Larry (Mr. Orville's son) and John Jr. (Jerry's daddy)!

The next thing he told me about was one time in the 1960s when Mr. Jim Hanes, who founded Hanes Hosiery (later to become the Hanes Corporation), owned Dews Island in Jarvisburg with the Chathams. John Wright Jr., Jerry's daddy, was the superintendent of Dews Island Club for the Chathams and the Haneses.

Mr. Jim told John Jr. one day that he was going to build a plant in Currituck to give the people in Currituck jobs. John Jr. said, "That would be mighty nice of you, Mr. Hanes." He went back to Winston-Salem and told his marketing people to do a study on the labor market in Currituck. They made the study and went back and said, "Mr. Hanes, it will take one thousand people to do a five-hundred-person job in Currituck because, if the fish are biting or the ducks are flying, they are not going to show up for work." End of plant.

What triggered this conversation between Jerry and I was that I was telling Jerry that my daddy told me that, one time, Mr. Cleveland Aydlett had a man come to see him about a job on the farm. Mr. Aydlett asked the man, "Have you got any nets?"

"Yessir, I got two or three."

"Sorry, I can't use you," Mr. Aydlett said. That's known as "Currituck time." I was telling this story about Mr. Aydlett to a member of Piney Island Club, Chuck Wall, and he too said, "That is Currituck time." That put me to thinking.

I have to admit I've lived my life on Currituck time. I guess that is why after having Currituck Realty for thirty-eight years, it's still in a trailer instead of a big office building like the offices of many of my competitors who have been in business many years fewer. There is one thing about it though: if I don't wake up in the morning—I've enjoyed my life on Currituck time.

Visit us at
www.historypress.net